OUR
INDEPENDENCE
AND THE
CONSTITUTION

★

by DOROTHY CANFIELD FISHER

Illustrated by ROBERT DOREMUS

RANDOM HOUSE · NEW YORK

TENTH PRINTING

Text copyrighted 1950 by Dorothy Canfield Fisher
Illustrations copyrighted 1950 by Random House, Inc.
All rights reserved under International and
Pan-American Copyright Conventions
Published in New York by Random House, Inc.
and simultaneously in Toronto, Canada by
Random House of Canada, Ltd.
Printed in the U. S. A.

CONTENTS

PART I

PHILADELPHIA

1776

CHAPTER I

PHILADELPHIA'S
WELCOME

THE FIRST CONTINENTAL CONGRESS HAD SENT A POLITE
letter begging King George not to listen to bad advisers
but to give his loyal and faithful American subjects
the general rights of all free British subjects. Also
those specially granted in their charters. To show that
they meant business, they had said they would wait a
fair time for a ship to cross the Atlantic with their
petition and to come back with the answer. If the British
government did not promise to do what they asked, they
agreed that the next step was for the American colonies
not to buy anything from England or sell anything to
England. That idea had worked, almost ten years before, with the Stamp Act. British merchants who did a
very profitable business with the Americans had lost a
lot of money when the colonies stopped trading with
them. They protested loudly. The Stamp Act was re-
pealed. The Americans hoped it would work again.

Then, in October 1774, the delegates to that first
Congress had gone home.

3

Now, six months later, on May 10th, 1775, they were coming back to Philadelphia to take part in another Continental Congress. But this second one was going to be very different and ever so much more important.

For, only three weeks before that date, Paul Revere had galloped at night from Boston, shouting his warning, "The Regulars are out!" By dawn on April 19th, red-coated British soldiers at Lexington had fired on American Militia. By ten o'clock in the morning, British soldiers had fallen back from American troops at the North Bridge in Concord. By dark that night, the British forces had retreated on the run to Boston, chased by Massachusetts sharp-shooting Minute Men.

For years now, Americans and British had been arguing and disputing, more and more angrily, about whether American colonies should take orders from the English King and his Ministers and friends without any say-so of their own about what the orders should be. It had been like water in a tea-pot on a hot stove, first simmering, then boiling, then sending off a long stream of scalding steam from the spout. The news of the actual fighting at Concord was as though the cover had finally blown off with a tremendous bang.

There really was something almost exactly like a loud explosion in the news that ordinary Massachusetts men in their everyday work-clothes, snatching up their muskets as they raced out of their homes, had not run away, scared, from the terrible British Regulars, but had stood up and fought—and won. For years, the English King and his friends had said, over and over, that the colonists were cowards. Maybe they had enough spunk to fight naked savages, but on the battlefield they would surely lie down and curl up. The Americans would "run like rabbits," so the London newspapers kept saying, if they ever saw real British soldiers in battle line marching against them.

Now all America knew. As the news from Lexington went racing through the colonies like wildfire, people cheered and shouted in relief and joy. And because they now knew that trained army soldiers and officers are not always better fighters than citizens, they saw the door to their future swing open.

All America knew and all America rejoiced, those who wanted to go on being English subjects just as much as those who wanted to be independent of England. For, that spring of 1775 when the news from Lexington and Concord came in, there were plenty of colonists who wanted to remain Englishmen. But they threw their hats into the air and cheered just as loudly as anybody else over the news that ordinary colonists really had fought against English troops. What they wanted was to be subjects of the English King, but also to have the King run the government by English law.

And the man who was King in England in those days wanted to act as kings did in France or Prussia—just the way they felt like acting, that minute. He didn't actually break any laws. The English Constitution stood up in front of him like a fence. But most fences have holes in them. The King was getting through the holes. He still went through the motions of doing the legal thing—such as having a Cabinet of Ministers, (like a committee to make plans) of rich, well-known English lords whose advice he was supposed to take. He took their advice, all right, as long as they advised him to do what he already wanted to do. But if any member of his Cabinet didn't say "yes" to his every idea, the King saw to it that he lost his job as Minister. He not only dismissed him, he made life miserable for him afterwards—for him and for his whole family, when that was possible.

Americans had been saying "no" to the King. But it was harder for him to make life miserable for Americans. For one thing they were pretty far away from London. And for another most of them earned their own living by doing something useful. They didn't, like many of the English lords and their families, depend on the King for soft jobs with big salaries and little work. He had grown more and more angry with the Massachusetts folks, who kept saying "no" to him, and had ended by sending to Boston ten thousand regular soldiers of his wonderful army that everybody in the world was afraid of. If the Massachusetts people wouldn't say "yes" of their own accord, he'd make them. And if he could make Massachusetts people give in to him, he could do the same thing to the other colonies any time he took a notion to. This meant that if he could and if he did, the people in the American colonies would be like prisoners in a jail. They'd have to do what the armed guards told them to, no matter what.

So if you'd been an American in 1775—whether you were one of those who wanted to cut loose from England altogether, or one of those who loved the best of English ideas and ways, and wanted to go on living under English law—you too would have jumped up from your chair at the news from Lexington and Concord, and shouted for joy.

Philadelphia people usually took things quietly. They didn't take the news of the fighting at Lexington and Concord quietly. Their hearts were bursting with feelings too big for words. But there are other ways than words, often better ways, to say what is hot in your heart. That May in 1775, a month after the fight at the bridge in Concord, Philadelphia found a way to give a tremendous shout of pride and hope and courage, without speaking a single word.

This is what they did. The first delegates to that important second Congress were due on May 9th. Philadelphia, in 1775, was the biggest city in America, twice as big as Boston; but by the day after the news had come in that it had been British, not Americans, who had "run like rabbits" on the retreat from Lexington to Boston, there was scarcely a single one of all the thirty thousand people in the city who did not know that on May 9th their town was going to give those delegates a welcome nobody would ever forget.

The morning of the 9th, out on the road where the travelers were to come in, several hundred armed men on horseback stood waiting, their band in front of them. They had sent lookouts farther along the road to catch the first glimpse of the approaching delegates and gallop back at top speed to say they were coming. The mounted men on their fine, shiny-coated horses stood ready in taut, straight ranks stretching a long way down the country road. The band players in front, also on horseback, fingered the keys of their trumpets, blew softly into their flutes and fifes to be sure they were in tune, held their drumsticks poised over the tightly stretched drum-heads. The horses tossed their heads, their well-oiled hooves glittering as they shifted their feet nervously. They knew beforehand how loud that band was going to sound when it broke loose.

Ahead of them, the pleasant, tree-shaded earth of the country road stretched empty and waiting. They were

all straining their eyes to see the messenger hurrying
back. Before there was anything to see, the bandmaster's
sharp ears caught the rapid pulse of a gallop. *"All
ready!"* he shouted warningly to the band.

The bandmaster brought down his arm. The band
burst out into that thundering crash of brass and drums
which the horses had known would come, but which all
the same was so loud that they flung up their heads,
their manes tossing wildly.

"Forward *M A R C H*!" cried the officer in command.

They stepped off to the blaring music of the band.
At the turn of the road, ahead, a little group of
travelers on horseback came into sight.

They drew rein, surprised, not knowing what their
part in the celebration was to be. How would they know
what to do? They sat their horses in the road a little
uncertainly. But they had no reason to be uncertain.
Everything to the last step had been planned out beforehand.

Just before the noisy band reached them, the command "Halt!" was given. On a one-*two* beat, all the
marchers stopped at the same instant.

"Present AR-R-Rms!" sang out the officer in command. The swords flashed out. Holding to this salute of
honor, the band and the first half of the company
swung their horses about to the command of "About
F A C E".

The other half of the company divided in two lines,
drew their horses to each side of the road. The band,
tootling and braying proudly, their horses stepping

high, passed between these lines. The first detachment of
the company marched after them. Then those who made
up the side lines, their bare swords still held in the
salute of honor, moved forward, went past the travelers on horseback, and wheeled to the center of the road
behind the men they were welcoming.

The maneuver was over. An advance guard of honor
now marched in front of the delegates, and a rear
guard of honor behind them. What the travelers had to
do was plain. They sat up straighter in their saddles,
pulled the skirts of their riding coats down more
smoothly, and felt of their cocked hats to be sure they
were straight on their heads. Then they started their
horses forward, trying to look as though they were used
to being met by hundreds of mounted men and a band
every time they took a ride.

But that was not all. They had not gone very far
before they saw, looking down the road past their
mounted advance guard and band, long lines of soldiers
on foot, infantrymen, and riflemen. They too were standing at attention, presenting arms. They too had a band
of their own banging away for dear life, not to be out-
done by the troops on horseback.

The same maneuver was carried out as with the
mounted welcomers. The foot-soldiers divided, fell again
into line at the head and at the rear of the company.
Their band now marched at the end, and the procession
was so very long that their music didn't interfere with
the mounted band bang-whanging away at the front.

In the middle rode the delegates. And soon they had

In the middle of the procession rode the delegates

to try harder than ever to look natural and easy, for as
they reached Philadelphia, there were more people looking at them than some of them in all their lives had
ever seen together.

All the delegates came from smaller cities, some from
the country, where a few hundred people was considered
a real crowd. And on that May 9th, 1775, at least half
the population of Philadelphia was out on the streets
to welcome them. Fifteen thousand people dressed in
their best clothes stood crowded together, bursting into
cheers, "Hurrah! Hurrah!" when the little group of
riders came along in the middle of the guard of honor.

Now the bells began! Above the loud hurrah!-hur-
rahs! which half drowned out the two brass bands, every
steeple of every church in the city began to clang joyfully.

The horses stepped proudly, the drawn swords of the
riders glittered, the infantry swung forward in time to
the whirling music of whichever band was nearest to
them. The crowds in the streets grew thicker and
thicker, they cheered more and more loudly, their hearts
beating faster in the uproar. After a while, the shouts
were not only "Hurrah, hip-hip-hip-hurrah!" but *Lexington! Lexington! Concord!"*

By this time, the delegates being welcomed into the
Second Continental Congress were as excited as everybody else. They forgot to feel embarrassed at being the
center of all the celebration. Their faces were flushed,
their eyes were shining. They were a part of all this.

Everybody there was a part. And the whole was something bigger than any of them had ever dreamed of. The women in the crowds lining the streets waved their handkerchiefs, the men waved their hats, they all cheered and cheered—their feelings far beyond what could have been put into any words.

But it was being said! It was being said by the steady tramp, tramp, tramp of marching men, by the clatter of prancing horses, by the trumpets, the thundering drums, the squealing fifes, and the shouting voices of thousands and thousands of people.

The delegates were as carried away as anybody else. Some of them had tears of excitement in their eyes. Bang-whang! Every throb from the drums was a heart-throb for all those people, every trumpet note was a hurrah!

The procession wound on and on through the crowded streets and finally turned into Chestnut Street. Before the fine Pennsylvania State House (we now call it Constitution Hall), they drew up in a formation which left a broad lane open for the delegates to the front door of the big brick building.

Men sprang forward to hold the horses. The delegates dismounted, walked forward, and mounted the steps. As they did, the noise rose to a hurricane, the church-bells flinging down their loud, brazen sound-waves, the drum-sticks rolling furiously on the drums, the trumpets and the shouts rising to the clouds.

The delegates turned on the top steps, took off their hats, bowed to the crowds. The doors opened. They walked in. The doors closed behind them.

The welcome was over. All the Philadelphia people were proud that it had gone off so perfectly. Not a detail wrong. They were proud. And they were tired. You can't be as excited as that without being tired afterwards.

The horsemen and foot-soldiers did an about-face and marched away. The crowds of men and women and children hung around for a while getting their breath, looking up at the closed doors and windows behind which the meetings of the Second Continental Congress were to be held. Then they too drifted away to their own homes, to live it all over again in talk. Although nobody had spoken a single sentence, every one of them was deeply satisfied, the way you feel when you have had a chance to say your say all out.

The street outside was empty, except for the men holding the horses of the delegates, a wandering cat or two, and some small children who chalked out a hop-scotch game and began to hop around its squares. They had already forgotten about the parade which, of course, they hadn't understood any more than the cats did.

Inside the Assembly Hall, cool and quiet after the streets, the delegates stood wiping the sweat from their foreheads and necks, or dropped into chairs to get their breaths. Unlike the cats and the little children, they knew perfectly well what the welcome-parade had meant. And they knew that it was very serious business. Some of them were rather pale. Those who had sat down took off their hats and held them on their knees.

"A warm welcome, sir," said one to a man near him.

The other nodded. "Yes, very fine. Very fine," he agreed. "I had no idea that the people here felt so united on this question. Do they, in your province?" he asked.

A third delegate spoke quickly. "I wish everyone in my province of Delaware could have heard those cheers. But I shall write back about this. They must know."

Two men walking past this group stopped. One of them said, "Was that not a noble welcome!"

"Very fine," said the other. "All the same—all the same——" He paused.

There was a silence. Then a tall, ruddy-faced man called across the room, "You mean, I take it, that although the welcome was joyful, what is before us here is not joyful, but the hardest kind of hard work."

There was another silence. Then the first man said, "Well, no, Colonel Washington, I wasn't thinking of hard work. Rather that things have now gone beyond loyal petitions to the King. We've other things to do, and—fine welcome or not—we may, every one of us, be hanged for our part in this—if we don't succeed."

This time there was no silence. Several men spoke at once, quickly, all in the same words. "But we *will* succeed," they said.

CHAPTER II

COLLECTING
DELEGATES

THERE HAD BEEN PLENTY OF BOYS AND GIRLS AMONG the thousands of Philadelphia folks who had stood cheering and shouting when the delegates to the Congress arrived. And there were plenty of youngsters among the crowds who, for months afterwards, walked slowly as they passed the State House, or stood in front of it in silent groups, watching the delegates arriving for a morning session or leaving when the afternoon session was over. Everybody knew how important the Congress was to America, everybody was anxious—some people were very much frightened—about what was going to happen. Little else was talked about in Philadelphia.

Naturally the children felt this; not the younger children, of course, who weren't old enough to understand or care about anything but play. The five- and six- and seven-year olders went right on running their legs off in tag or hide-and-seek or jumping rope. They were like kittens or puppies. You know how small children will tumble round, playing with each other, even when their folks are afraid the house is burning and are shouting for the fire department. But older ones, the smart ones, from maybe eight or nine years old on, had sense enough to know from the very tone of their grownups' voices, let alone what they said about Congress, that something serious and not-to-be-forgotten was going on in Philadelphia. They listened to as much of their elders' talk as they could hear. They asked their parents questions when they didn't understand. They looked hard, as their fathers and mothers did, at the men from other colonies, delegates to the Congress, whenever a glimpse was to be had of them.

If it was near time for a session to end, the youngsters hung around in front of the State House waiting for the big doors to open and the delegates to come out, to go back to the boarding-houses or the hotels where they were staying.

The delegates usually looked tired. Sometimes they looked glum and downcast. Sometimes they seemed excited. Sometimes they were just serious, and walked slowly in little groups. A boy or girl could stand staring at them, and they'd never notice. Their faces, often troubled, often anxious, sometimes pale, sometimes deeply flushed, turned towards each other as they talked.

A year is a short time for grownups. For children it can seem to stretch on forever. Philadelphia children saw those delegates to the Continental Congress coming and going to the State House for more than a year before anything exciting—exciting for them, that is, like the Welcome Procession—happened again. When it did happen, it was so much more important than any shout-

ing and marching and band-playing parade that you'd hardly believe it. In fact it was, many people think, the very most important thing that ever happened to Americans.

But for long months, Philadelphia streets were quiet. The older boys and girls came to recognize delegates from other men because their clothes somehow didn't look just like those of Philadelphia people, and because they were nearly always so serious-looking.

You could tell a delegate from your neighbors but there wasn't much to help you pick out one from another—except for a few. Everybody soon came to know Dr. Benjamin Franklin because he was so old, and Mr.

Thomas Jefferson because he looked so young. And Mr.
John Hancock, President of the Congress. Or no, you
didn't come to know John Hancock but rather the style
he put on. Such style! It was as good as a show to see
that great coach of his go by. He was inside it somewhere, of course, but all you saw of him was a flash of
expensive clothes through the window. Your eyes were
taken up with his four servants, tricked out in fancy
uniforms like dressed-up monkeys (so disrespectful
people used to say laughingly) mounted on splendid
horses with gleaming saddles and bridles. And before
and behind that great carriage clattered a sort of guard
of *fifty* men on horseback, each one with a sword, not
pushed down into its leather case, but bared and flashing
in the light.

"Whatever in the world makes Mr. Hancock do so
much show-off business?" people would ask each other,
and someone would always answer, "Oh, the Hancocks
were poor folks till his uncle's time. He wants to be
sure everybody knows they have money now."

The Philadelphia children soon had him on their list
of Congress members whom they recognized on the
street. They were "collecting delegates" the way modern
children collect pictures of baseball players or movie
stars.

They soon recognized Dr. Franklin by sight, too, because nobody who had seen that old man could ever forget him. Especially if they'd had the good luck to see
Dr. Franklin smile. There was something like sunshine
about his smile and the way his keen old eyes softened.

People spoke about that as much as about his being so celebrated, the most famous American alive, in fact the only famous one. Evidently Mr. Jefferson from Virginia liked the old philosopher too, for they were often together. The children who lived near Dr. Franklin's house sometimes watched as the simple little carriage carried the stout old man to the State House. But on fair days, when it was neither too hot nor too cold, they saw the old doctor trudge home on foot, leaning on young Mr. Jefferson's arm.

Once a tiny little girl who lived on Dr. Franklin's street looked up from the sand pile where she was playing and saw that the short, broad, stooped old doctor and the slim, tall, young delegate had stopped beside her. Smiling pleasantly, Mr. Jefferson leaned down to pat her head. "I have a little daughter at home, just about your size," he said. "She has hair just the color of yours. Her name's Patty. What's yours?"

"Debby," said the child, not much interested. People were always saying they had little girls at home "just your size."

But after they had walked on, Debby's two big brothers came pelting out from their house to say, "That was Mr. Jefferson and old Dr. Franklin! They *spoke* to you. Don't you ever forget that!"

They were shocked to have little Debby say she didn't know either of them. They told her as best they could themselves, although when it came down to facts they found they didn't know as much as they thought. The children in any other house on their street would have asked their parents to tell them some more. But Debby's brothers didn't. There was a difference of opinion between their mother and father about the Continental Congress and what it was doing.

C H A P T E R   I I I

E A G L E   F E A T H E R S
A N D   T O M A H A W K S

Most PHILADELPHIA FAMILIES THAT YEAR TALKED POLI-
tics for breakfast, lunch and supper. But not in the
house where little Debby lived. When an express rider
brought in a piece of political news which raced
through the city, Debby's mother looked worried and
said nothing. Debby's father didn't seem worried a bit,
but excited and eager. He looked as though he had a
lot to say. But he never did say a word, because he
didn't want to hurt his wife's feelings.

Once in a while his sons wanted to ask him to explain something they'd heard at school or in a school-
mate's home about the long dispute between the colonists
and the English King. But they knew better than to ask
him where their mother could hear them. They watched
to see him coming home, and ran to meet him a block
away from the house. But then he didn't answer much.
He told them briefly what the facts were, and added,
"Now your mother wouldn't want me to get you to take
sides. She thinks so much of her Cousin John, you
know. It's her idea that you're too young, anyhow. So

let's not talk about it now. Perhaps later on, some time."

"Cousin John" was Mr. John Dickinson. He was one of the Pennsylvania delegates to the Congress. A very fine man, so everybody said, even those who didn't agree with him about politics. Well, it would be hard, so Debby's two brothers thought, for anybody to know how to agree with him. It made them dizzy even to try to understand what he did want. Yet he wanted it so hard!

With all his heart, as hotly as John Adams wanted America to be entirely independent of England, John Dickinson wanted to remain a loyal subject of King George. That's what he said. He meant it, too. But what he did was to vote money for more American militia, to do his level best to make America strong to fight, exactly as if he were on the side of Independence. He hated a real out-and-out Tory, whose idea was to take off his hat and make a bow and accept anything the King wanted to hand out. If Cousin John Dickinson met a British-minded person like that, he flew into a rage, just as John Adams from Massachusetts did. Yet he always disagreed with Mr. Adams, and often very angrily.

The boys' mother, who knew her cousin well, said his point of view was easy to understand. He wanted to remain a loyal Englishman. But just *because* he had British ideas, he wasn't going to be ordered around by anybody who didn't have a legal right to. He wanted an Englishman's full rights. His idea was, she said, that every Englishman knows you have to stand up for your rights if you're not going to have them taken away from you. Englishmen in England always had stood up for their rights. Look at their standing up against King Charles First. If Englishmen in America showed that they were ready to fight for their rights, they wouldn't have to. Cousin John felt that all this elegant writing by Mr. Jefferson, for instance, about freedom and tyranny and what-not, sounded to Great Britain like just talk. "What the English government has always taken seriously and always will," he used to say, "is strength, not words. Make a fine speech about your never being willing to have your law cases tried in a court where the King has chosen the people in the jury, and nobody in the English cabinet pays any attention to you. Reach for a loaded musket as you say it, and they'll give in peaceably to your reasons—if your reasons are good. And ours are good. They'll see we mean business. The stronger the colonies are in weapons and men, the surer we will be of getting our legal rights from England. It's always been that way with Englishmen. It always will be."

Just once the boys' father told them, after Cousin John Dickinson had been at the house talking like this, "Your mother's cousin is a fine man, but he doesn't realize that the man who is now King of England is more German than he is British. It hurts him so when anybody doesn't agree with him he fairly yells with pain, the way a man yells with a toothache. The old English way was to respect people who disagree with you, if they are strong and reasonable. But King George hates such people! The stronger they are, the

more he hates them, because it makes him think for just
an instant that there *might* be a possibility he couldn't
always get his own way. And *that* idea seems to drive
him just about crazy. But there, run along, boys. Your
mother wouldn't like to have me talking to you like
this. You are her sons as much as mine."

The boys got into a way of hanging around outside
the front door of their house about the time their
father was due home. They'd pass a ball back and forth
or play jack-stones. But the minute they saw their
father turn into the street three blocks away, they'd
race to get to him.

"What's the news, Father, what happened today?"
they'd ask him in low voices, after they'd reached him
and were walking back, one on each side of him.
Sometimes he didn't know any specially interesting news
items. Sometimes the news was bad. That winter the
American troops were fighting in Canada, trying to capture Canadian cities from the British, and they were
terribly beaten. Just didn't get anywhere. That was
terrible news.

Sometimes the news was exciting. Their father's voice
was full of feeling on the days when he told them
about one and then another and then another of the
American colonies, where the British governor, ap-
pointed by the King, had left his office and taken ref-
uge on an English warship. The people in those colonies—the everyday people—were now voting for their
own governors, were choosing for themselves the men
they wanted to run the government, instead of having

to take any man the King wanted to send them. Connecticut people, for instance, had declared themselves no longer a British colony but a State, an American State, "under the sole authority of the people thereof, independent of any king or prince whatsoever."

"Now don't speak of this to your mother, boys. It would make her feel badly. It's not what her Dickinson cousin would like."

He himself evidently liked it fine. He said the words as if he loved every one of them. And another time, he choked up and had to stop talking for a minute because his heart was so full. This was when he had heard some young men from South Carolina talking about the

day on which their newly elected governor—elected by
the people's votes, not sent from England—and their
assembly, also elected, marched to their State House.

"The South Carolina men told us the big crowds
that gathered to watch the procession go by couldn't
even cheer. They just stood 'in a kind of rapture,' men
and women alike, to see, marching to music behind
their escort of uniformed cadets, 'their *own* rulers,
chosen by *them*, men they knew and loved and trusted.
And men they themselves could vote out of office if
they didn't do the right thing!' Those young men from
the South said that they themselves stood on the sidewalk as that procession went by, and cried like children. Wait a minute, boys, let me get my handkerchief. I don't want your mother to be asking me if I
have a cold in the head."

The boys never forgot the time—this was early in
the year, in March—when their father told them, very
much astonished, that the ten thousand red-coated British troops who had been in Boston all winter had sailed
off to Canada.

The boys could hardly believe their ears. Everybody
had been afraid of what all those soldiers might do.

"*Why?* What made them go?" they asked their father.

"Well, the American troops got hold of the big cannon from Fort Ticonderoga, and put them on a hill
across the water from Boston, where they could fire right
into the city. But the British were about ready to leave,
anyhow. Starved out."

"But—but—but——" cried the older boy, "I thought

the British Regulars could beat *any*body. Why did they *let* the Americans get the cannon up on the hill? Why didn't they march out and beat the American soldiers and just grab the food they wanted?"

"I can't imagine why not," said their father. "I don't know why any more than you do."

"Maybe the British Army isn't as good as they say it is?" ventured the older boy.

"Do you suppose that could be?" their father wondered. "It *does* seem very queer that they just backed off from the American militia and went away. And I can't understand, either, why the English government didn't send in from England food and muskets and gunpowder to stand by their own army shut up in Boston. They could have done it easily. The harbor of Boston is open to the sea. They've got all the ships in creation. I can't make head or tail of it. But it sounds mighty good to all Americans. Unless there's a catch in it somewhere."

They were at the house, stopped talking and went in together.

It was understood between them that they were not to mention in the house these brief snatches of talk with their father.

But one piece of news they all enjoyed together, their mother as much as anybody else. It seemed good to be talking something over with her, too. It was a relief to have her proud and happy over *something* that had happened.

One day their father brought back the news that the Congress had sent a special message to the Indians, asking them not to act as enemies to the English, not to attack the English if there should be fighting later on. They didn't ask them to support the Americans. The message said something like this: "What we are asking you for is *Peace*. This is not your quarrel. If it comes to fighting, the quarrel is between the colonists and Old England. It's not *your* fight at all. What we ask of you is keep the hatchet buried deep."

The boys' mother talked a great deal about this. She told them to be proud of being English, not French. The French King had, she said, in those long-drawn-out French and Indian wars, *paid* the Indians good money to fight on his side. "The savages were paid, so I've always heard," she said, "a high price for every American colonist's scalp they could bring in. And, although the French probably didn't actually tell them to kill and scalp American women and children, they did. Once Indians get into a fight, they just can't be kept from murdering anybody in sight. It was horrible —the way everybody in the colonies anywhere near the Indians was afraid of those sudden Indian raids. A party of them would swoop down on a poor little village, yelling and shooting, *with some French officers in command*. Wouldn't you have thought they'd have been ashamed, men from a civilized country, to let wild savages kill little girls and boys?"

"Now you see, boys," she always ended such talk, "how people act who are brought up in the English ideas of right and wrong. *Our* people *ask* the Indians *not* to attack *anybody*."

Congress did more than ask. They voted money to buy presents for the Indians to persuade them not to get into the fight. And, to the intense delight of Philadelphia children, after a while the six big Iroquois tribes sent word that more than twenty of their chieftains would go to the Continental Congress to thank the Americans for their gifts.

It was too good to be true! Debby and her brothers and her father and mother were as excited about this thank-you visit from real Indian chieftains as if they were all children together.

Their father found out the day the Indians were to come, May 28th it was, and which streets they would pass along to get to the State House. He said he'd take the morning off, and go with his family to see them.

Bright and early that day they stood waiting to see the Indians go by—along with crowds and crowds of other Philadelphia people. Everybody was glad to have something like a show going on besides Mr. Hancock's absurd guard jingling by. As for the other delegates, it was not much of a treat for anybody to see those quiet, serious, unlaughing, middle-aged men.

"Mother, did you ever see Indians, real ones?" asked the boys as they waited on the sidewalk.

"Yes, once," she said. "When I was your age, I was taken to visit some family connections who lived 'way back country, in the woods. There were a few Indians around there. But they weren't much to see. Dirty, bad-

The Indians . . . went by like shadows

smelling men in old, ragged white-man's breeches and coats, with nothing more Indian-like than maybe a band of scarlet calico tied around their greasy black hair."

The boys were disappointed. "Do you suppose these Indians will dress like that?" they asked.

Nobody knew. Not then.

But they did, half an hour later. From far away down the street came a low, dull, slow, but somehow loud, *throb, throb, throb*. It was a drum. Different from any drum they had ever heard. It was as if somebody hidden and behind your back were telling you, "Look out! Something's going to happen! Something dangerous to *you!*"

People pushed the children into the front line so they could see. Everybody leaned forward and looked down the street.

Now, mingled with that dull throb from the drum, came a strange, dry rattle, like bones shaken together.

They were coming. Even from a distance you knew why people were afraid of them. Their copper-colored bodies were bare to the waist and painted in great staring patterns of many colors. With their every move their muscles rippled close under the skin—as they walked, as they breathed, as they swung their arms—so that the lines of the painted patterns stirred, writhed, seemed to be alive.

They wore short kilts and leggings of pale tan, smoked buckskin brilliantly decorated with bead-embroidery which twinkled, flashed, caught the light in red and green and yellow and blue sparkles. Long belts

fringed at the hanging ends. Villainously sharp toma-
hawks thrust through those belts. And what foot-gear!
Solid embroidery made of flat tiny quills, all colors
woven in and out in patterns no white person knew
how to make.

Over each head floated a single great eagle's feather.
An elaborately decorated deerskin quiver filled with
feathered arrows hung from the left shoulder to the
right hip, across their backs. Most of them carried long
heavy bows. Some of them had in one hand a rattle
made of turtle shells which they shook lightly in a
faint, ghostly rhythm as they passed. Several wore leg-
bands with dried deer-hooves hung closely together,
dangling and rattling with a horrid little noise unlike
any other.

A gasp of wonder over these strange and gorgeous
costumes went up from the Philadelphia crowd in their
drab, substantial, gray and brown clothes and thick-
soled, practical black and brown shoes. But as the Indians went by, treading soundlessly in their soft-soled
moccasins, silence fell on those American colonists, the
silence of respect—and fear.

The bright-colored embroideries, the threatening,
muffled sounds from drum and rattles—they were forgotten once the warriors came stepping by, their thin,
bleak faces focused on something far, far away. They
might have been walking, each by himself, on a lonely
path in the woods. The sight was never forgotten by the
children who, that day, gazed up into those high-nosed,

stone-like, copper-skinned faces with the long black locks hanging on each side.

Not only the children shrank back from those great savages. The grownups, too. What strange eyes those were, hard, jet-black, cold, not noticing, not even seeing the staring people, the Philadelphia battalion drawn up to impress them. They were mighty fighting men, every one of them. But they went by like shadows, with a step as noiseless as a deer's.

People forgot they had come out to see a show. They stood silent, almost shy in the presence of such alarming power.

On the way home the boys said not a word. Their mother too was silent. She took their father's arm, and walked very close to him. He carried little Debby. She, who usually chattered like a chickadee, clung to him and hid her face on his shoulder.

When they were once more in their own living room, their mother slowly took off her bonnet. She was thinking hard. "They are like great serpents——! How *could* the French——!" she murmured, and gave a shudder.

The boys were startled by the expression on her face. It was not just that she was very pale. She looked—could it be that their mother looked as though she were afraid?

They had never thought she could be afraid of anything. That day when they were little, and the big dog set upon them fiercely in the street, their mother had been like a lion. She had flown to them in one great rush, had dived in, and caught that animal by the scruff of the neck, shouting at him in a voice that actually made him slink off. But now she looked sick with fear.

Their father set little Debby down, stood up, went to put away his hat, and said heartily over his shoulder, "They make that stuck-up John Hancock look like a brass penny, don't they?" (But he looked anxiously at his wife.)

After a glance up at the familiar picture of King George over the mantel, their mother finally saw a way to tell her sons what she tried to tell them about everything that happened. "Now boys, you see what you have to be thankful for, that you were brought up on *English* ideas."

CHAPTER IV

COMMON SENSE

THE SNATCHES OF TALK THE BOYS HAD WITH THEIR father were short. And he always reminded them he didn't know about anything for sure. Especially about what was going on in the Continental Congress. The delegates had promised not to tell anybody about the discussions—whatever they were—of the Congress. Of course everybody wondered, guessed, speculated, gossiped, and then passed on to his neighbor these guesses and rumors. Yet everybody knew well enough they could only guess.

But boys as young as Debby's brothers didn't know enough about discussions and committees even to make much of a guess. They saw those soberly walking (all but John Hancock in his coach!), quietly dressed delegates go into the State House mornings, fresh from their night's sleep, and come out hours and hours later. By that time they were so tired that they looked, as people used to say in those days, "as though they had been drawn through a knot hole." But what, the boys wondered, did they *do* all day long, every single day except

Sunday, all through the hot summer, and the mild Pennsylvania autumn and the dark winter days, and the spring again, almost summer? The boys just could not imagine what those men found to do all that time, behind those closed doors, sitting round in chairs, talking and talking.

Their father always told them he didn't like to discuss politics in the home, because he and their mother had such different ideas, and he thought the world of her. Yet the children knew their parents couldn't keep off the subject which, that year, filled everybody's thoughts. They knew their father and mother *did* talk about it together, for after they had gone to bed, they often heard those two voices going on and on downstairs in the living room. But since the day they had had that dispute about *Common Sense*—well, it wasn't perhaps a real dispute, but it came as close to that as anything that had ever happened in that home—the boys had known their father didn't want *them* to get their mother started about independence and King George III, and the Continental Congress, and all the rest that was being discussed over and over in everybody else's house.

What had happened about that book was this: one morning in February, the master of the boys' school walked into the classroom reading a little paper-covered pamphlet. He laid it on his desk, but as he took off his hat and heavy coat, he leaned over it, reading fast, as though he couldn't stop. And then, sitting down, he raced through a page or two before he re-

membered where he was and called the school to order.

The boys near his desk craned their necks, of course, and caught a glimpse or two of the pages. They did not look a bit interesting. No pictures. No conversation. Just solid fine print, like a school text-book. And when he finally closed it, they could read the title— *Common Sense!* Of all things to get excited about! Yet all that day their teacher, every minute when he was not busy with a class reciting a lesson, snatched the little book up and read in it. While they "did" their arithmetic problems, they kept flicking quick glances at him, because as he read his face grew flushed, his eyes sparkled and blazed. Several times he laughed out loud, and once he clenched one hand into a fist and brought it down, slam! on his desk. It made them jump.

And how it did make them want to know what was inside that dull-looking book with that dull title. "Common sense" was something your grandparents lectured you about, and very tiresome they made it sound. How could it make a long-legged, lively, smart young man like their teacher (he was teaching school to pay his way while he studied to be a lawyer) get red in the face, laugh out, clench his fists and forget where he was?

They were on pretty good terms with him—for a teacher—and before they went home that afternoon, they gathered around his desk to ask him about the book.

"Oh, did you notice I was reading something?" he asked them, surprised.

"Tell us about it! Can we read it?" they asked. "Will you read it to us?"

He thought for a minute. Then, "I declare I don't know," he told them. "Your parents may have different ideas from mine." He hesitated. "I tell you," he suggested, "you ask your parents this evening if they're willing to have you read *Common Sense*. Then you tell me, tomorrow morning. I'll lend it to any boy whose folks say he may read it. You don't need me or anybody else to read it to you. It's easy—reads itself—like somebody talking to you."

"But how can we ask them if we don't know what it is about? How can they know what kind of a book it is, if you don't give us some idea?" they asked him.

To their surprise, he laughed as heartily at this as though they had said something foolish. "You'll find your folks will know about it, all right," he told them.

And *did* they! That evening at the supper table the older of Debby's brothers said, "Say, Father, Teacher was reading a book today, called *Common Sense*——"

Their mother dropped her knife and fork on her plate with a clatter. "Did he read that book *to you?*" she asked in a really awful voice.

No, no, they assured her. He had been reading it to himself, and they noticed he seemed all taken up with it, so they asked him if they could read it. And he said to ask their families if they could.

"Certainly not!" said their mother. "You're much too young. I won't have your minds upset."

The boys turned to their father. He shook his head. "I don't want you children to go against your mother's wishes," he told them. "If she doesn't want you to, you'd better not. The book really is for grownups anyhow."

"Now listen," said their mother seriously, "I want you to promise me you won't look inside that book. You always keep your promises, I know."

"But how would we ever have a chance *to* look inside it," they asked bewildered, "if we're not allowed to see Teacher's copy?"

At this, their father and mother looked oddly at each other. And the boys got the idea that there was a copy of the book in the house that minute. After all, if their mother hadn't read it, how would she know, at the first mention of its title, that she didn't want them to read it?

Their father said, smiling a little as though there was a joke they didn't know, "You *may* see other copies. Your teacher may not be the only one to have the book."

"But, *Mother*——" they began imploringly.

Their father said quickly and a little sharply, "Now boys, I want you to promise. Your mother does everything in the world for you. It won't kill you—just not to read one book. It'll be right there for you to read later on, when you're older. Now promise."

So they did. They thought a lot of their mother, and they knew she was having a hard time just then, for she hated to disagree with their father.

They kept their promise, too. As their mother said, they always did. But it was hard. For in a few days that little paper-covered book seemed to be everywhere. They knew why their father had been amused by their thinking their teacher's would be the only copy they'd see. It seemed to grow up out of the ground, like grass blades, sprouting by the hundreds. Every house had it. People read it as they walked along the streets. Newspaper articles about other things would suddenly say, "As *Common Sense* remarks,——" The man who lived next door leaned over the wall between the two

back yards and read a piece out of it to their father as
he was planting the peas. In the bakery, or at the
green-grocer's shop when their mother sent them on
errands, they heard people talking about it.

So although they did not once look inside it (till
their mother gave them leave to) they couldn't help
knowing some of the things that were in it. Since
they did not see the words, they didn't get them just
the way they were printed. But they got the sense of
those sayings. Nobody who'd once heard them could
forget them. This is the way they remembered some of
the things people were quoting to each other that
winter:

"In England a King hath little more to do than to
make war and hand out easy jobs for rich people to
make them richer. A pretty business, for a man to be
allowed four million dollars a year for that—and to
expect to be worshipped into the bargain!"

"Trace back a king's forefathers—the head of his
family was always the strongest thief in a band of
robbers."

"England calls itself our 'mother country!' Not
much! Europe, not England, is the father and mother
of America. This new world hath been a safe home for
people from every part of Europe who want to live in
Freedom."

"England hath given Freedom warning to depart. Oh,
America receive Freedom, and prepare a place for men
to live in liberty!"

Well——! They knew now why their mother didn't want them to read that book! But she was wrong about its upsetting their minds. It didn't. It seemed to settle them, rather. And their father said it had settled his.

C H A P T E R   V

REPORT TO DEBBY

OF COURSE AFTER THEY HAD SEEN THEIR MOTHER FLY
off the handle that way, they were even more careful
about not saying a word about the news of the day
when she was around. But they kept on talking to each
other, and to their schoolmates, about how one British
colony after another, all that winter and spring, was
voting itself into an American State. Like their father,
they felt proud of each new State governor, chosen by
the people, not sent from England to do what the King
told him to.

At the table they talked about the weather, and lame
Aunt Ann's rheumatism, and wondered when the first
strawberries would be ripe in their garden. But by
themselves, they kept on wondering aloud about the do-
ings of the delegates to the Continental Congress. What
did those men do, all day long, they asked each other?
What went on behind those closed doors, week after
week? With almost every colony declaring itself independent of England why didn't *they*—representing all

44

the colonies as they did—do something like that for the whole of America?

Their little sister Debby was often playing around near them as they talked together. But they paid no more attention to her than they would to the cat's being there. They forgot that she could understand words.

Debby had heard her brothers say the same thing so often, that by the end of the first year after the delegates had come to Philadelphia the words had stuck fast in her memory like a counting-out rhyme. She knew it the way you know a nursery rhyme—hickory-dickory-dock.

She had a mixed-up idea that what her brothers said so often had something to do with the stout old gentleman in dull-colored clothes who sometimes walked slowly past her home to his own house. And with the slim, elegantly dressed young gentleman who had a little girl at home named Patty, just about Debby's size. The old gentleman had been away—up in Canada, she had heard people say—for many weeks, and all that time the tall, younger one had not gone along her street. But now that it was summer, they sometimes went by together, old Dr. Franklin dreadfully lame, leaning all his weight on Mr. Jefferson's arm.

If you have had kid sisters or brothers, you know how every once in a while, they'll break out, saying or doing something that surprises everybody. You don't know what gets into them. One day in June, when little Debby saw the two delegates coming near, she laid her doll down on the grass and ran to meet them, calling out, "What do you do, all day long, every day? What do you *do*?"

The two men stopped, astonished. Then they laughed. Mr. Jefferson sat down on his heels till he was Debby's size and asked, "Say that again, Debby, won't you?"

Debby was much too young to feel shy, and anyhow everybody liked Mr. Jefferson. So she repeated it, looking straight at him, her blue eyes wide. Dr. Franklin said, smiling, "Tom, Debby's other name must be echo. What she asks must be an echo of what everybody is asking."

Mr. Jefferson stood up. "What in the world can you

tell an infant like Debby?" he asked, stroking the silky hair that was like his little Patty's.

But if Mr. Jefferson was a father, old Dr. Franklin was a grandfather, who knew twice as much about youngsters. He pointed to a stone mounting-block near them. (In those days all houses had a mounting-block of stone or wood to help people get up into their saddles.) "Debby, climb up, will you, dear, so you and I will each be as tall as the other, and I'll tell you something."

Debby scrambled up like a squirrel and stood there, her blooming little flower-face on a level with Dr. Franklin's. He took her tiny hand in his wrinkled knotty old fingers.

"You're too little to understand *now*," he said, "and if you were the Archangel Gabriel we couldn't tell you, not *really*, because we've promised not to. But we can give you an idea. If you'll be here when we pass by tomorrow afternoon, I'll have a report for you."

Mr. Jefferson lifted the little girl down and shook her hand. "Don't forget," he said. "Tomorrow afternoon."

The two delegates walked on. Debby went to pick up her doll. She meant just to go on playing "keep house." But out of the house came her two big brothers. "For goodness gracious *sakes*!" they cried. "Whatever in this world did you say to them? And whatever in this world did they say to you?"

"Why, I asked them what they do, all day long, every day? And they said they'd tell me tomorrow."

"We don't believe a word of it!" cried the boys, and took Debby in to put it to their mother. They thought she wouldn't mind, even though it was sort of politics, since their little sister was in on it.

She was as much astonished as they. She thought, as they did, that Debby was so little she'd probably got something twisted.

"I believe I'd better be out there with her tomorrow afternoon," she said. "I'm afraid my little girl has been forward. I don't want her to bother people, even if she didn't mean to."

"Oh, Mother, Mother, may we be there too?" the boys asked.

"Why not?" she said. "If you're quiet, and mind your manners."

So the next afternoon, it was all of Debby's family—except her father—who stood there with her when Dr. Franklin and Mr. Jefferson came along. Debby's mother had made them practice their manners. When the delegates were near, she herself spread out her wide skirts and bowed low in a dipping curtsey, as ladies did in those days. The boys bent over from the waist in the kind of bow that was the style for men and boys. Debby wore long full skirts too. All little girls did. Her mother had showed her how to spread them out to make a curtsey. But just as she took hold of them, old Dr. Franklin smiled. It was his good, grandfatherly smile. His pale, wrinkled old face looked desperately tired. But his smile was like sunshine. Debby forgot her

manners and ran to him, her arms wide open—clasping
him around his knees.

The two gentlemen took off their cocked hats, bowed
to Debby's mother, gave a friendly nod to the boys. Mr.
Jefferson said, holding out a piece of paper, "Here,
little miss, is our report."

Things were written on the paper—letters and figures.
Debby ran back to her mother with it. "Oh, read it to
me! Read it to me!" she cried as though it were a
story.

"Yes, do, madam," said Mr. Jefferson. "The paper is
for a little American to keep. It will explain, perhaps,
what will come later."

He swept his three-cornered hat off and made a fine
bow. Dr. Franklin felt in his pocket, brought out
a piece of sugar-candy and slipped it into Debby's
hand. They went on. Debby's mother stood with the
paper in her hand, blinking her eyes as if she had been
dreaming.

"What's on it, Mother?" asked the boys.

"I'll go into the house to read it," she said, "where
I can be quiet."

Inside the house, she read the paper through to herself. When she had finished, she looked doubtfully at
her sons. "I don't know what to do about this," she said
in a troubled voice.

"Oh, let us see what's on it," cried the boys.

Debby had wandered away, her doll in her arms. As
she sucked on Dr. Franklin's sugar-candy, she thought
that was much the best part of what had happened.

"I don't know whether I ought to," said their mother.

"Oh, Mother, why not!" they begged. *"All* the other boys' folks tell them about everything. Why shouldn't we——?"

She folded the paper together. "We'll wait," she told them. "I'll talk to your father about this. I don't feel the way he does. About any of this."

She looked at her two sons. How tall they were growing. She hesitated. "Are you old enough?" she wondered, "to have us talk to you about——?"

"Mother!" cried the older one. "I'm fourteen, going on fifteen."

"Well *you* are, maybe," she said, as though she didn't like to admit it.

"Mother!" cried the younger one. "Who do you take *me* for? Debby?"

She put the paper into her pocket. "We'll see what your father says," she told them.

CHAPTER VI

UNDER THE PEAR TREE IN THE GARDEN

THEIR FATHER CAME HOME RATHER LATE FOR SUPPER, as he often did in those days. The boys thought he looked tired and worried and yet excited. He often looked so, that June. Little Debby had had her bowl of bread and milk and gone to bed. She and her doll were sound asleep. Supper was eaten quietly, the boys having agreed not to tell their father about the "Report to Debby" till he had had his supper and lighted his pipe. They waited till they had all gone out to the walled-in garden plot back of the house, to sit under the pear tree in the mild, Philadelphia early-summer evening.

When their mother, with a nod, gave the boys leave to say what they were bursting to tell, their words tumbled over each other.

"Take turns, take turns," said their mother. "First one, then the other."

They told their story, cried out, "We want to *ask* you about it!" stopped, out of breath, and looked at their father.

"Let me see this paper," he said, holding out his hand. "As you tell it, it's nonsense. The delegates are under the strictest orders not to let a word of their proceedings——" He held out his hand. They gave him the paper.

He read it all through carefully, laid it down on his knees, took his pipe out of his mouth, and turned to his wife. He spoke gently as they had always heard him speak to their mother, but he said something they had never heard him say before. "Don't you think, Wife, that boys as big as ours ought to know what's going on?"

The mother said earnestly, "They're your sons as much as mine. I won't go against your wishes. But I want them to hear what I think, too."

The father nodded. "Yes, you and I will take turns, first one and then the other. That's fair play." He turned his eyes on the boys very seriously. "But listen," he said, "no nonsense about this. I'll answer your questions as well as I can, but it's no book-story! I won't guarantee you'll find it interesting. It is little children like Debby who don't need to listen if they're not interested. But big boys like you—why, both of you may soon be carrying muskets."

The mother cried sharply, "No, I can't bear that!"

"It's my turn," said the father. "Let me speak first. Then you can say what you want them to hear. First of all, I'll read them what's on this paper. You could have done that. What's on it is only what everybody knows about any gathering that's conducting any business.

"Dr. Franklin probably thought of this as a little piece of foolery to amuse Debby. It's said that he spoils his grandchildren terribly, and that their mother can't do a thing with them since their grandfather came back from England. He lets them do whatever they like—if they make him laugh.

"Such men wouldn't write anything that wasn't perfectly correct. And they haven't. . . . Yet to make a playful keepsake for a little girl, they've made an official looking paper out of it with their two names signed."

He read out:

"Report to a young American on the kind of work done by the Second Continental Congress, all day long, every day, as she says. Set down in the month of June, 1776 for Debby, by two fellow Americans slightly older than she.

"Every day, about two-and-one-half hours spent listening to letters from the Colonies . . . reports on their status."

The father laid the paper down a moment to say, "The word 'status' means how they are getting along. Of course we all know that reports are received. We've eyes in our heads. Express riders come and go all the time, and every stableboy knows where they come from."

He read out: "Report to a young American . . ."

He went on. "Often, of late, debate on the best means
to comply with General Washington's request for longer
enlistments."

The father sighed. "We know that too—worse luck!
For a while last winter, so many three-months-militia
soldiers went home that the General could hardly find
men to hold his lines before Boston."

He read on from the paper:

"Lengthy consideration of the state of our Treasury . . . after which we vote:—

To authorize purchase of muskets for one battalion,
and " " " " uniforms provided the
cost be deducted from the soldiers' pay.

To authorize payment of $23.00 for cartridge
making.

To authorize payment of $12.00 to nurse for sol-
diers with smallpox.

We listen to reports from various committes, such as
Service of the Constitutional Post.
Saltpeter.

Ways and Means to Protect Trade of the Colonies.
Board of War and Ordnance.

"You see, my dear child, many things concern *all*
the United Colonies, not just Pennsylvania and Virginia, and such things we, the Congress of those United
Colonies, have to take care of. We are trying to run
your country's business for you just as your mother runs
your home. Dull, tiresome details are always part of the
work of government, as of housekeeping. They must be
thought about, and talked about, and decided honestly

and promptly, even though they are not at all interesting.

"Remember this, my dear child, when you are a
woman grown and living under a free government of
your own people." ("Whew!" thought Debby's brothers
"Cousin John Dickinson wouldn't like that!")

"The great things do not come by themselves. They
are built up by working hard to solve the tiresome little
problems which come up, day after day."

Respectfully submitted,

B. FRANKLIN

T. JEFFERSON

The father laid the paper down on his knee, took up
his pipe and said, "Now boys, what is it you want to
ask me?"

The younger one had his question on the tip of his
tongue, and got it out before his brother could open
his mouth. "What in the world is saltpeter? Why should
the Congress have a committee about that?"

Their father found this an easy one. "We must have
gunpowder. It's made of three things mixed together—
charcoal, sulphur, and saltpeter. Anybody can make
charcoal. And sulphur isn't hard to get. But saltpeter——! It's hard to find. And to make. There *are*
places where it is found in the earth. It can be bought
from such places. But it costs a lot.

"Now, England has any amount of money. The same
year they got hold of Canada from the French, they
also got hold of India. India is a big, rich country.

Lots of money comes into England from there. More than that, England is full of manufacturers, and they pay taxes by the hatful. The King can get plenty of money to buy saltpeter anywhere in the world. But we can't."

The older boy asked, "What kind of manufacturers are those in England that pay so many taxes?"

"All kinds," said the father. "Woolen goods—iron works—plating mills. Hats."

"Why don't we have them manufactured here in America, and get taxes from them?"

"Because the British government won't let us," said their father promptly. (But he didn't look at his wife.) "Their idea is to keep us from manufacturing things for ourselves. That would make us prosperous. They don't think anybody should be as prosperous as people born in England. Take hats—beaver hats are all the style. There's lots of money in manufacturing them from beaver skins. All the beavers are on this side of the Atlantic Ocean. None in England. Americans are 'allowed' to trap the beavers. But if we make hats out of the fur, we are not 'allowed' to sell them where the British hatmakers want to do business.

"And take wool. Our wives and mothers are 'allowed' to spin and weave homespun cloth inside our own homes. But if you live in Pennsylvania, you are not 'allowed' to sell a yard of it across the river in New Jersey. And of course none of it must be sold in England, or Holland, or France. The English woolen-makers want to sell in those countries. There's money in selling good woolen cloth. So only the English can do it.

"And iron foundries. The English are glad to have us send heavy bar-iron across the ocean to them. Just rough iron isn't worth much. Then they make all kinds of useful things out of our iron and ship them. We could do it here as well as they. But they make laws to forbid it to Americans.

"Take nails! The first step is to cut big chunks of iron into little pieces in a slitting mill. The pieces can be made into nails in home forges. Our farmers would like to do this in winter. But the British law forbids our setting up any new slitting mills. So our countrymen have to sit idle when farm work is slack. British manufacturers can make money out of nails, so nobody else must be allowed to do it."

The boys' mother spoke now, in a low murmur, "I'm only a homebody, but I know as well as you that there is a lot of iron work done in Pennsylvania."

"That's true," admitted their father, "and there are lots of hat factories in New England. And all of them, if they were started since that British law was made, are illegal." He turned to the boys. "Your mother isn't in manufacturing, of course, and never has been, so she doesn't know what crooked business a man is forced into who runs a factory forbidden by the law. There are, of course, certain officials who ought to report you. You have to bribe them not to do it. You have to bribe anybody who threatens to tell on you. The officials you bribe, have to bribe others to keep it quiet. It means dishonesty in everything you do. It means the whole machinery of enforcing the law gets rotten. And why? So that British manufacturers can make money.

"Now to go back to saltpeter. Dr. Franklin is one of the finest scientists anywhere. I'm pretty sure he is on the committee to see what can be done about saltpeter. I hear too that up in New England some of their best people are working on that problem. If we can't get salt-peter, we're beaten before we start."

The older boy held up his hand to ask a question. "That Committee to protect the trade of the colonies—why should it have to be protected?"

His father laughed, shortly. Not at all as if he found anything funny in the question. Rather as if it rubbed him the wrong way. "Not much chance of protecting it, as things stand nowadays. We haven't got much to protect."

"What's the matter with it?"

"Well, in the first place, the British government has never 'allowed' us to trade with any country but England. We have never been 'allowed' to—" (the boys noticed that he said the words "never been *allowed* to" as though they made a bad taste in his mouth) "buy anything direct from France, or Holland, or Italy. Yet people in those countries make lots of things we'd be glad to buy of them. The English government has always 'ordered' us" (here the boys saw the same bitter-taste expression on his face, although he spoke quietly) "to buy everything through English merchants. *They*

could buy wherever they liked, and they were very glad
to sell to us. Of course at a profit. Almost any profit
they wanted, since we have to buy from them."

Their mother still said nothing. She was knitting a
pair of stockings for Debby and kept her eyes on her
work.

"And now it's worse," their father went on. "They've
gone further. They used to 'allow' us to trade only with
them. But now the King, since he is so angry with
Massachusetts and all the rest of us Americans, won't
let *any* trade go on, in and out of our ports. Last winter
he had a new law announced, saying that we are
rebels and that nobody, anywhere in the world, is to
buy anything from us or sell us anything, or he'd consider *them* enemies. In the same announcement he told
the world that any American ship could be captured at
sea by anybody who wanted to capture it, and its cargo
taken and its sailors made prisoners, and *he* wouldn't
care, because he had no use for us. As long as we keep on
being British colonies, there's nothing we can do about
that. But, if we declare ourselves an independent country——"

The boys looked quickly at their mother, as if the
father had said a bad word aloud. She was pale, she
looked terribly sober, she murmured "They'll never,
never vote for independence," but she played fair and
let their father have his turn first.

"——we can buy things from anywhere, except
England, of course, and sell them to any country. I sup-

pose this committee to protect the trade of the Colonies has something to do with that."

The older boy reached over, took up "report to Debby," and ran his eyes over it. "What's this about a Board of 'War and Ordnance'?" he asked.

His father hesitated a moment and his mother laid down her knitting. "Boys, I think *my* turn has come to speak. I don't know what the word 'ordnance' means. But I do know what war means. That Committee is working to get everything ready to make war on England. What for? Your father has been explaining the reasons. Because we think they are making more than their fair share of money. Because we think we could make more money if we were independent of them. Just business. But decent people don't try to kill each other over money. They get in the lawyers—not the gunmen. Your father doesn't take a loaded musket downtown and shoot a man because he's making more money than we are—even if your father thinks he is not exactly fair. He tries his best under the law to make the man do the right thing." She spoke quietly, with no excitement.

Their father said, "Oh, my dear girl, I'm so glad you feel we can talk this over together. With our sons. It's been a sorrow to me to have anything between us that we can't talk about. I'm glad our boys can hear us, and find out that people can have different ideas and still not be angry with each other."

He put his hand on hers and asked, "May I go on?"

She nodded, her eyes on his. She dropped her knit-

ting in her lap. Just before he spoke again, she said
with deep feeling, "Our Congress will never vote for independence. That would mean war. It won't come to
shooting. It can't. There are too many good folk in
England who don't want war any more than we do." She
was almost crying.

Her husband said, gently, "Yes, so there are. But just
now, in these years, our kind of people in England
don't have—so it seems—much to say about running
their government. And we *have* war, now. The shooting
started last April, in Lexington and Concord. And in
June at Bunkers Hill."

"We must keep it from spreading beyond Massachusetts," she said in a low voice. "The King will send us
people to make peace, not war—*if we are patient*. That
is what Cousin John Dickinson keeps saying. If we show
we are in earnest, they will send people to get all these
tangles straightened. I expect every day that express
riders from New York will come in with that news."

Her husband thought a long time before he answered
her. "Your Cousin John Dickinson is a fine man. He is
sure that we could, if we would only go on trying, get
together with the English people. But we can't reach
the English people. Between us stands this King. He's
managed to get the government entirely into the hands
of his friends. And they all have the same idea he has—
or they wouldn't be friends of his."

"What is his idea?" asked the older boy.

"It's what's called 'personal rule'. That means 'The
King is the master'. It's a very old idea that was given

up in England long, long ago—that ordinary people who work every day for their livings should have mighty little right to say what their government does. The King wants to go back to the old, old days, centuries ago, when anybody who could get himself on a throne felt he could do whatever he pleased. He's very stubborn, and he's kept at it and *kept* at it, till now he's got the government in England under his thumb.

"Your mother isn't quite fair in saying that what we are ready to fight for is only the right to make more money. It's the right to live under law—not under some man's orders. And we think that law is made by everybody's getting together and deciding about what has to be done."

Their mother said, "But the King has *said* that he is going to send over some fine, upright people to make peace with us."

"That's what we *heard* he said," answered her husband, "but what did he do? Sent over ships with cannon and attacked Falmouth in Maine and Norfolk in Virginia, places with no forts, no artillery to fight back —just a lot of homes with families in them—and burned those cities to the ground. And his orders were—we know this, for sure—to attack our seacoast cities 'at that time of year when it would most distress the people who live in them'."

His wife looked sad, did not contradict this, murmured, "We must be patient. There are always misunderstandings. It is wrong to take for granted that a misunderstanding——"

"There's no misunderstanding about the King's hating us," said her husband, his voice rising a little. "He hates us because we stand for everybody here or in England or Scotland who won't give in to him on everything. He hates us, and we are where he can get at us, not mixed up with everybody else, as his subjects are in England and Scotland. It won't be people to make peace with us he'll send over. He'll send—why, the talk around town is that he's going to pay thousands and thousands of foreign soldiers to fight us!"

His wife cried out, "What nonsense! The English people would never let the King do such a thing."

"He's got them where they can't help it."

"That's the craziest story I ever heard!" exclaimed

his wife. "Why, the whole quarrel started about his ways of getting money from us to pay our share of the costs of the French and Indian wars. He wouldn't pay out millions of tax-money——"

"I keep hearing people talking about it," said the father.

"You can hear anything," said his wife.

"Yes, it does sound like wild talk, like something invented," admitted the father.

The younger boy yawned. Their mother's eye caught this. She stood up. "There, that's enough for tonight. More than the boys can take in now. They can't understand politics at their age."

"We can too," said the older one. "Sort of, anyhow." But he also could not keep back a yawn.

It was dark. A little moon showed through the branches of the pear tree. They went back into the house and each one lighted a candle to carry up to bed. On the wall, King George's face looked out at them from the place over the fireplace where his picture had always hung.

CHAPTER VII

DEBBY'S MOTHER
CHANGES HER MIND

AFTER THE TALK UNDER THE PEAR TREE, DEBBY'S TWO big brothers felt themselves almost grown-up. Their father treated them more like men. He talked to them more about the danger of British ships some day appearing in the river, close at hand, and shooting up Philadelphia as they had shot and burned down other American cities. He told them more about what he was doing, serving in the guard set to protect Philadelphia.

On the evening of the last day of June, their father asked them to take a walk with him. Their mother took for granted that they were just going out for a stroll, leaving her to put little Debby to bed.

When they started off, the boys thought so too, but as soon as they were out of the house, their father said, in an anxious voice, "Now boys, there's something on my mind. I want to ask your advice about it. Let's go around to those benches near the State House yard. We can talk there without anybody hearing us. It's about your mother. I'm worried."

This gave the boys a scare. Their mother had always

done the worrying about them. Could she be sick? That would be terrible. She always took care of them when they were sick. When they came to the first bench, they sat down on it, and looked hard at their father.

From their father's first words, they saw that his worry about their mother was just another piece of their difference of opinion. "You know," he said, "what your mother thinks about England, and how Americans ought to act."

Yes, the boys said, they knew how their mother felt.

"That evening under the pear tree, you remember how she simply would not believe that the King might pay foreigners to fight in the English Army. She said it was foolishness to think he would take millions of dollars from the British tax-payers to *buy* himself an army to get the better of us Americans, when what he wanted —what he *said* he wanted—was to get back some of the money he had already spent on us. She said it was just talk. Just gossip. She said you could hear anything."

Yes, the boys remembered that very well. The older one said he thought his mother was probably right. It *did* seem unlikely the King would spend so much more money than what he had wanted to get from Americans in the first place.

"Well, he's done it," said their father, in a heavy, desperate voice. "Your mother hasn't heard the news yet. But it's all over town. It's not just talk any more. News has come in from General Washington himself that more than a hundred British ships—oh, many more than a hundred—have been sighted coming into New

York harbor. Lots of them are warships, armed with cannon. They could shoot New York city right off the map. And Philadelphia too. If they could get up the river.

"Those that aren't fighting ships are transports—full of soldiers. A *big* army. The biggest that ever crossed the Atlantic. The English soldiers are regulars mostly, paid professionals. Such troops fight to earn their living. They'll attack anybody any time, anywhere, because that's their business. But the King hasn't nearly enough professional soldiers to put down the Americans. So he's taken in thousands of Highland-Scotch and Irish troops. In the place where those people live, everybody is kept so very poor, the men have to take any jobs they can to keep from starving."

He took a long breath. "And boys, nine thousand hired German soldiers are landing. And ever so many more thousands coming in later. The King will pay more than fifteen million dollars to those German kings or princes before he gets through. He's going to bring over thirty thousand Hessians. More than we have in all our American armies put together. He'll pay *any*thing (only of course it's not out of *his* pocket, it's tax money paid by the British people) and do anything, to punish Americans because we have wanted to have our fair legal rights, as the British law gives us rights."

"Oh, what'll Mother *think!*" exclaimed the older boy.

"Will she have to know?" asked the younger.

"Of course she will. She'd have known by now if she were a man, out doing business on the street. Every-

body's been talking about it. But that's not all———"
He paused, took off his hat, wiped his forehead, swallowed hard. "There's something worse."

The boys were petrified. What could be worse?

"At least those Germans are soldiers. They fight other soldiers, not women and children. They don't scalp people. But the King is going to turn the savages loose on us, too. He's going to give the Indians leave to burn American homes and murder American families, to help him get the better of us. The *English* King! And he used to talk so against the French for having the wild Indians fight beside them and murder white settlers. What will your mother think?"

At the idea of what their mother would think, the boys were too shocked to speak. They stared silently at their father. How could they bear to go home after their mother knew this? She would cry her eyes out. Why the other evening she was almost crying at the very idea of anybody's being against the King. They had never seen their mother weeping. She had always been the one to help her children keep back the tears when something was the matter.

"Do you suppose Mother will cry?" asked the younger boy in a whisper.

Their father nodded, sadly.

There was a long silence, broken finally by the older boy saying in a low shamed voice, as if he were speaking of something that nobody should mention, "Mother was very, very frightened of those Indians when we went to see them. She looked terribly scared."

Their father nodded again. "All American women are afraid of Indians. Why wouldn't they be? And your mother—especially—— She never told you this, but one of her uncles who lived off in the back country was murdered in a French and Indian raid. And all his family. His wife and three little children. Of course your mother's scared of Indians. We'll have to try our best to make her feel that it's not likely they'll ever get as far as here." The twilight dropped slowly around them, like a thin blue veil.

It was almost dark when the father drew a long breath and stood up. "I wanted you to know this, boys, before your mother did, so you could stand by when she has to hear the news. We're three men together. We'll have to be good to our womenfolks. It's natural for them to be more afraid of things than we are, and to have their feelings hurt more. I don't say that my feelings aren't hurt by the King's wanting to get the better of us so much that he'll do such things! But of course my feelings are nothing to what your poor mother will feel. I just wanted to give you boys a chance to get your breath. I knew you'd be taken aback by this. I thought we all three could be more of a comfort to your mother if you knew beforehand."

The big bell in the State House tower slowly and seriously struck eight.

"We'd better go back now. But remember, boys. Not a word to your mother. She shouldn't know till she has to, poor girl."

They halted in their tracks, too appalled to move

On the way home, none of them said a word. They went slowly. They were not anxious to reach the house.

As they approached it, they saw that candles had been lighted in the front room. And the curtains had not been drawn together! Their mother always drew the curtains or closed the shutters before she lighted a candle. Everybody did in those days. Through the unveiled windows they could see that someone was pacing rapidly to and fro in the room. Startled, the boys ran to fling open the door. What they saw froze them, half in, half out of their home.

Their mother was not sitting down with her mending, as she often was, after Debby was in bed. With long steps, she was striding away from them, her back to the door. She heard them coming, and spun around to face them. How tall she looked! They had never seen her look so tall.

The instant she saw them she began to speak. They would not have known her voice. It was like a trumpet sounding a call. Yet it was not loud. They halted in their tracks, too appalled to move.

"While you were gone, news came in," she told them in that strange, low, sharp voice that sent shivers up their backs. "You must hear it too. Express riders are in from New York. They say an enormous fleet of British warships has come into that harbor. They are bringing a tremendous army. All the British regulars who were shut up in Boston. Other regulars. And thousands and thousands of German soldiers! More than a million dollars of British tax-payers' money is to be paid for their hire."

Her voice deepened, darkened. "And the King, our English King, is not just sending soldiers to fight our soldiers. He is going to use the wild Indians to attack us, just as the French did."

She was trembling now. Her burning eyes showed that it was from anger, not fear. "It makes me *ashamed*," she cried, "to have been a subject of a King who will do that. Why, what have we done to have him want to burn our houses and slaughter our children! We have disagreed with him about taxes. The quarrel is about *money*! Would I, if I could, send shrieking bands of Iroquois along the country roads in England, to scalp the women and butcher the babies, just to get the better of them in a quarrel about *taxes*! I'd die before I would. And so would any decent person."

She flung back her head—she towered up taller. "The King won't even read our petitions to send people to arrange this in peace. But he answers them. His answer is to send in the biggest army that ever crossed the ocean to kill us, and the biggest fleet to burn what's left of our seacoast cities."

She flung out her arm and cried, "He thinks he can *scare* us into taking less than our legal rights. Why, he's just a bully!"

Stepping close to her husband she cried, "Now we must never give up, never! Never! Now the Congress *must* vote for independence. Now they will!"

She turned to her sons, who were gaping, frightened by her, but stirred to their hearts. "Boys, *nobody* must *ever* give in to a bully because he has a big club! This is more than a quarrel between two countries. It's between what makes life worth living, and what makes you ashamed to be alive. In that fight, if the bullies come out on top just because they are strong, it will be shame, shame for everybody—everywhere, forever! Never forget that, my sons."

They ran to her now, they put their arms around her. She felt as strong as a pillar. Over their heads, she said to her husband passionately, "If I could, I'd shoulder a musket and go out to fight alongside you."

The boys were horrified. "Oh, Mother, somebody's got to stay home to take care of Debby."

She drew a deep breath. Her face changed. She said in a low voice, "Yes, somebody must stay with the little children."

In their arms, she turned back into their mother —not a voice like a trumpet, not a tall, strong pillar, just their mother. The boys found they'd been too excited to breathe, and now drew in a deep long sigh.

"Well——!" said their father. He hadn't even taken his hat off yet. He did now. Holding it in his hand, he bowed before his wife, lifted her hand in his, and kissed her fingers.

She looked lovingly around at their three faces. It was as if she hardly knew what she had been saying. She tried to smile—she always smiled when she looked at her family. But she could not smile. Not yet. She had something else to say. She spoke very earnestly, but not in that fierce low voice which had scared them. "You're thinking I'm going back on everything I've told you before. Not a bit. I don't want to fight the English nation, and they don't want to fight us. If *they* were the ones who wanted to fight us, this army landing in New York would be made up of enlisted Englishmen, not of starving Highlanders and Irish, of professional soldiers and Germans. The very reason the King has to *buy* himself an army is because his own people won't fight us. Never forget that, boys."

She looked now, as she sometimes did when she'd been sick, pale with dark circles under her eyes.

"Sit down, dear girl, sit down," said her husband.

She did sit down in her own small armchair, where the boys had so often sat on her lap when they were little. How good it looked to see her there again.

But she had one last thing to say.

"Nobody knows what's before us," she told them. "We may not often be together by ourselves like this. There is one other thing I want you to remember, no matter what comes. When we are threatened by a bully, why do we flare up and stand fast instead of being afraid and giving up? It is because our forefathers came from England. It's not against the English people I'm ready to have my country fight. It's *for* them. If the King has got them down where they can't flare up and stand fast, as they always used to, he hasn't got us Americans down. If these are years when they can't fight—as they did a hundred years ago—against a

King who wants to run the government all by himself, well, we'll do it. It's our turn."

Now she had said everything she needed to say. Like the boys she began to breathe deeply and rapidly as if she had been running. A little color came back into her face.

The boys and their father sat down too. It seemed a lot longer than one short hour since they had left that room for their talk on the bench—that familiar home room.

But something was different about it. Something was changed. Dazed and shaken, they looked vaguely around them. Nothing could have changed in such a short time.

Their mother was speaking to them again. They turned their eyes back to her. She was looking at them and now this time she really saw them. She said, "Mercy! It's 'way past your bedtime. What are we thinking of! You won't get good marks at school tomorrow. Be off with you! Don't forget to hang up your clothes, and wash your feet, and say your prayers before you get into bed."

They went up to their rooms, clumpingly, their heavy shoes loud on the stairs.

As they reached the top, their mother called after them, "Boys! you might as well read 'Common Sense' now, if you want to. It's in the chest of drawers in our bedroom. Third from the top. Left hand side. Under my stockings."

As they undressed, one said to the other in a hushed

voice, "Did you notice—I didn't want to speak about it—but the picture of King George is gone from over the fireplace."

The other nodded. "Yes, I saw it standing, its face to the wall in the corner."

They gazed wide-eyed at each other, shook their heads and fell into bed.

CHAPTER VIII

LET FREEDOM RING!

SHE WAS RIGHT, DEBBY'S MOTHER WAS. THEY DID
vote it. But after a last wild flurry of excitement!
Philadelphia was now so full of talk about who was
voting which way in Congress, that nobody had breath
for anything else.

Not that anybody knew a thing, you understand.
As old Dr. Franklin had told Debby, the delegates
were not supposed to breathe a word about their discussions to anyone. And they didn't. Not really. But
everybody was so wrought up that news seemed to
leak out through the mortar and bricks of the State
House walls. A lot of what people kept telling each
other was not true, of course. Maybe none of it was
true, people would say to each other, even while they
were repeating what they had heard. But there was
plenty of rumor such as it was.

Everywhere they went, they heard reports—maybe
imaginary, maybe not—of what was going on.

"It seems a Virginia delegate had stood right up
there in the State House and moved that the Colonies

are, and of right ought to be, Free and Independent!"

"It was 'most a month ago he'd said that, but they haven't voted on it yet."

"It will be voted any day now."

"No, it won't. John Dickinson is working just as hard as ever against breaking off from England. He says he's ready to enlist in General Washington's army and fight for our legal rights. But no independence for him. He wants us to stay British. He's a stubborn man."

"He won't change. And I'll wager the other Pennsylvania delegates will back him up."

"Maryland's against it too."

"They *were* against it. Their legislature is meeting again. I've heard say they're going to send different instructions."

Then somehow, the word got around that John Adams of Massachusetts had made a wonderful speech in favor of independence.

Everybody knew that Mr. Adams was on that side. It wasn't any surprise to have him urge separation from Great Britain. What astonished people was his intense, burning feeling about it. He had been thought rather cold, by nature, although with lots of brains, and rather saving of his words. He often walked alone on the Philadelphia streets, always sober-faced and tight-lipped. People thought he was not friendly-looking. And he was a lawyer who, like most lawyers, was a good man in an argument. But this speech of his—so people said, wonderingly—was no argument with pros and cons. It was a fiery outpouring from his heart and head, of love for human freedom and hatred for what stood in the way of human freedom. Nobody could resist it. Why—it was said—the delegates were fairly lifted out of their chairs by it, cheering and applauding, yes, even those who'd always said they were going to vote "No".

"I don't guarantee this to be true, neighbor, but it's what I hear. They say he made John Dickinson with his cautious, British-leaning speech sound like a sick old cat."

"But Delaware is in a snarl. It has only two delegates in Philadelphia, and they take different sides."

"Now, Cousin Peter, we're all guessing. Nothing's known."

"But some say that their third delegate, Caesar Rodney, would vote 'Yes.' Then Delaware's vote would be two to one, in favor of independence."

"Maybe, but poor Rodney's a sick man, and eighty miles away down in South Delaware."

"No hope of getting him here in time."

But there was. An express rider was sent out with a letter calling him back to vote. And Caesar Rodney answered the call. He tied a green silk handkerchief over his face to hide the scars of his disease, and wore out four changes of horses as he galloped all night through the dark, over muddy roads, July thunderstorms rolling wildly about his head.

The little knot of watchers on Chestnut Street never, till their dying day, forgot the mud-spattered horse and rain-soaked rider, the tall, skeleton-thin man, his face masked up to his hollow, sunken eyes. He was so stiff with that tremendous ride that he had to be helped out of the saddle. For an instant he swayed on his feet. He almost fell. Then he went up the steps and into the door of the State House.

People turned to one another and said, "That was Rodney. Delaware will be all right now."

And how about Pennsylvania? Had anybody seen John Dickinson that day? Was he inside the hall? It turned out that he wasn't. Debby's mother had been wrong in thinking that Hessians and Indians in the British army would change his vote. But only partly wrong. Even now he couldn't give up his dream of convincing the King to grant the legal rights of Englishmen everywhere. He still had a vision of an America ruled with justice where no one would be taxed without representation; but it would be British justice. He couldn't bring himself to vote to break away from England. But in the end he didn't vote against independence either. He and a friend who thought as he did stayed away. And Pennsylvania, together with all the other Colonies, said "Yes." The Declaration of Independence was voted.

People still spoke of them as "colonies" more than half the time though that wasn't exactly accurate. All of them now by the will of their own citizens had declared themselves States . . . all except New York which hadn't quite finished doing that. But its "yes" vote was promised as soon as it too had finished chang-

Caesar Rodney . . . went up the steps

ing itself over from a British colony to an American State.

All thirteen were States, dependent on the votes of their own people, not on the King or his ministers. They could now join together as one nation, and as one nation declare to the whole world their union and their independence.

At last the people of Philadelphia could stop guessing. The great question was settled. The Declaration officially adopted was to be read aloud inside the high walls around the State House yard at noon. People began planning to be there early.

In Debby's home, the evening before that great day, there was a long discussion. The little girl was to be left at home, her parents said. Lame old Aunt Ann could come in to stay with her.

But Debby's brothers said she must go too. "Why, she's the one Dr. Franklin and Mr. Jefferson first spoke to. And now people say those two are the ones who've written the Declaration mostly. It would be too mean to leave *her* at home."

"But boys, what would be the *use* of taking Debby? She's too little to understand a thing of what all this means."

"Yes, *now* she is. But if we take her, she could always tell about having been there."

The father saw the boys' point. "There's something in what they say," he said. "It'll be a great thing for anybody to say—that he heard, with his own ears, the first public reading of the Declaration of Independence."

But in the morning Debby had another idea. She wanted her dolly to go too.

The boys thought this was too silly. "Oh, Mother! people will laugh at us if we had a doll along!"

"I don't believe anybody there would even notice," said the father, "whether a little girl has her doll. We'll be thinking of bigger things. Boys, do you *realize* that this is one of the most important things that ever happened, anywhere! History hasn't a record of anything a bit like it. And we're going to be there."

They set off early. Not any too early. The yard was big. But long before noon it was not big enough. The crowd grew denser. Debby's father held her on his shoulder. The boys stood on each side of their mother, each one holding fast to her hand, not to be separated from her. Around them people were inching themselves into less space.

Some time ago, a wooden platform had been put up in the Yard for looking at the stars. A rough little wooden building called "the observatory" had been left on it. And somehow Debby's family found they had been slowly pushed by the crowd into a position where their view was hidden by the observatory.

The boys felt that this was too much to bear.

"Now, Father! It's not *fair*! We were here first. We ought to——"

Their father showed them with a motion of his hand that nobody could move, not an inch, from where he stood. He said, "We didn't come to see, but to hear."

Just then a man behind them began to say something about the bell in the State House. The boys strained their ears to hear what was being said. "That bell was ordered from England to celebrate the 50th anniversary of William Penn's Charter of Privileges, more than twenty years ago. The foundries, when they cast bells, always have a text from the Bible to put on them. And what verse do you suppose was chosen to engrave around the edge of the bell that was coming to America? It was as if people knew about today—'Proclaim Liberty throughout all the land to all the inhabitants thereof.' "

As they gazed up at the tower, the voice of the bell sounded. Slow, dignified, stately, it rang for noon, twelve steady strokes.

The restless moving of the crowd had stopped. All those men and women were silent. The boys, pressed against their mother, felt her draw a long breath. They heard, as well as felt it, they were so close to her and the stillness was so deep.

Breaking this hush, came a loud inspiriting roll of drums. Not the dull throbs of those Indian drums. This was sharp, like the crackling crash of thunder close at hand which stirs the heart and shakes the roof tree.

Those in the crowd who could see were gazing at something going on to the accompaniment of the rolling drums. All over the yard, the men took off their hats and stood bare-headed. Debby's father and brothers took off their hats. They turned their faces toward the place where the speaker must be standing.

It was thus, standing motionless, gazing up into the blue, blue American sky, that they heard the Declaration of Independence—as a Voice, dropping down through the clear bright air, a strong, noble Voice, slowly, slowly pronouncing the great words one by one—the great words which were to change life for everyone there and for all their nation.

"When in the Course of human Events, it becomes necessary for one People to dissolve the Political Bands which have connected them with another, and to assume among the Powers of the Earth, the separate and equal Station to which the Laws of Nature and of Nature's God entitle them, a decent Respect to the Opinions of Mankind requires that they should declare the causes which impel them to the Separation.

"We hold these Truths to be self-evident, that all Men are created equal, that they are endowed by their Creator with certain unalienable Rights, that among these are Life, Liberty, and the Pursuit of Happiness."

At these words the boys, although their mother did not move at all, felt that she began to cry. They looked up into her dear face and saw her cheeks wet with tears. She looked down at them, smiled lovingly and pressed their hands.

They had thought it would be dreadful if their mother ever cried. They had never seen her so beautiful as now.

Other women around them were crying too. Silently, solemnly weeping, like their mother, they turned streaming faces up towards the beautiful deep Voice pronouncing those mighty words.

The boys lost the thread of what was being said, so shaken were their hearts by the sight of those weeping women, their quiet upturned faces shining through their tears of pride.

They looked at their father now, and once they had seen his face, they could not turn their eyes away. They knew his face well. But they had never seen it look as it did then. Years after, when they were old men, and their father long dead, they used to say to each other, "Do you remember how our father looked? He looked— like a lighthouse, with the lantern burning clear."

"I knew then that it was a lantern that no storm could ever put out."

One of them, trying to help his grandchildren understand a little of what had happened that day, told them, "Every man's face there was saying 'Amen! Amen! Amen!' to the words he heard."

What were those words? They found their spirits had been lifted so high and carried so far that for a time they could hear only that great trumpet of a Voice, not its words. They stood as in a dream.

They held fast to their mother's hands, not sure that they were still standing on their feet. They seemed to have no weight, no bodies. But slowly, dimly at first, then fast and strong, they felt again their own hearts beating. They remembered where they were.

They were listening to their nation's Voice. And now they heard its words*——

"We, therefore, the Representatives of the UNITED STATES OF AMERICA . . . in the Name, and by Authority of the good people of these Colonies, solemnly Publish and Declare, That these United Colonies, are, and of Right ought to be, FREE AND INDEPENDENT STATES; . . . and that as FREE AND INDEPENDENT STATES, they have full Power to levy War, conclude Peace, contract Alliances, establish Commerce, and to do all other Acts and Things which INDEPENDENT STATES may of right do. And for the support of this Declaration, with a firm Reliance on the Protection of divine Providence, we mutually pledge to each other our Lives, our Fortunes and our sacred Honor."

Those last three words, *"our sacred Honor,"* hung in the silent air. Then such a wild cry of jubilation broke out that for an instant they could not think what it was. Could that be the *bell*? Could that passionate *clang-clang-clang,* that topsy-turvy leaping into joyful tumult, come from the same bell that had so solemnly struck high noon! The Liberty Bell was ringing in their freedom!

As its shout burst forth, the waiting bell-ringers in the other churches, standing by, their hands on the ropes, flung themselves to work and began to pull for dear life. No musical chimes now. Just a joyful, joyful

---

* For complete text of the Declaration of Independence see page 183.

noise which sprang up above the city roofs with so powerful a leap it seemed as though you could see it.

The boys were beside themselves with excitement over the noise—the bell, the great bell over their heads, all the bells of the city pealing at once! There was another kind of noise, too, almost drowning out all that clamor. What was that?

Then they knew what it was. They themselves were shouting. Everybody around them was shouting with all his might. When had they begun to cheer? They did not know. With the last of those great words, they had burst into cheering as, with the first tug on its rope, the Liberty Bell had burst into full cry.

The crowd began moving. An outlet to the Yard was flung open. Those nearest them poured through it into the street. The pressure inside was lessened. The crowd thinned a little. Still cheering wildly, Debby's family was swept along towards the opening. Stepping fast to keep their feet in the rush, they passed close enough to the State House to catch a glimpse of it through the crowd.

"Oh see! *LOOK*!" cried the boys. A double line of delegates stood in front of the brick wall. They were cheering too. Their voices couldn't be heard above the tumult, but there they stood—those grave serious men, shouting with all their hearts, waving their hats in the air, the same light shining in their faces as in that of Debby's father.

The boys tugged at their mother's hands to make her see. "Look! Oh *look!*" they screamed joyfully to her,

"There's Mr. Jefferson! And Mr. *Adams!*"—for John Adams too—often so grimfaced and once in a while so cross-looking, stout, middle-aged Mr. Adams—was waving his hat wildly in the air and shouting "hurrah!", his face all brightness.

But Dr. Franklin—he was there, too, among the delegates who had come out to hear their Declaration read—what was he doing? As they were pushed along through the gate, into the street, they kept turning their faces back to make sure that they really saw what they thought they saw. The stout old man was shouting like everybody else, but was not just waving his hat. He had put it on the top of his cane, and was spinning it around and around, up high in the air, over everybody's head.

With one final squeeze, the crowd behind them pushed them along out of the gate into the street.

It was packed with people but there was room to breathe. They had shouted till they were panting, and now, wiping their foreheads and breathing deep, they began to come to themselves.

A man close to them (they never saw him before) said to their father, as if they were old friends, "Do you know—I could hardly believe it. None of that sounded new to me. It was just what *I* have been wanting to say. If I'd have known how to put it into words, I would have said just that."

The boys heard their father answer in surprise, "Why, *I* kept thinking that, too. It seemed as though I knew it all before."

He shifted Debby to his other shoulder. The boys dropped their mother's hands, and walked along behind their parents. They were back in Philadelphia again. How far away they had been! Now they were all just quietly going back to their own homes.

Before long, they turned into their street. One of their neighbors, a youngish man, his face working in excitement, came up to their father. "It was the strangest thing!" he cried out. "I thought for a minute that *I* was the person reading that! The words seemed to come from inside my own mind. I've wanted and wanted to say that, only I couldn't get it somehow clear in my thoughts."

"Now we all have it clear," answered their father.

Over and over on the way home, the boys heard people saying the same kind of thing. Not till afterwards, when people knew the Declaration from reading it in black print on white paper, did they ever hear anybody speak about its being finely written, or having beautiful language like music. On that day, what was felt by those who heard it was that it came from their own hearts and minds.

All the way home they heard pieces of the Declaration floating in the air. Their mother murmured to herself, " 'Life, liberty and the pursuit of happiness'— I'm so glad they put that last word in! Think of a government set up to help its citizens try to find happiness."

Their father saw a friend across the street and shouted out, "—'are and of right OUGHT to be free and independent'——"

His friend called back, " 'We hold these truths to be self-evident'——"

The teacher of the boys' school went by them, his long legs striding fast. He was chanting, " 'When in the course of human events'——"

What the boys themselves remembered was the last sentence. The younger one said aloud dreamily, " 'We mutually pledge to each other our lives, our property and our sacred honor.' "

"Oh, *not* 'property,' " cried the other, " 'our fortunes'."

"Means the same thing," murmured the younger boy, almost too tired to speak.

"Doesn't sound the same," cried the other.

They were close to their own home now. Just ahead of them, their next-door neighbors were turning in at their own gate. They were good friends and the two families stood together for a while to talk over the event.

"Did you ever think you'd see this day?" asked Debby's father.

"No, I did not. I can hardly believe it now. I must go right in and write my old grandfather about it. He's ninety-two and his grandfather fought with Cromwell against King Charles the First. He's said right along, old as he is, that we'd have to come to this. He said Cromwell had taught kings they are just men and not gods, and that's what English people would always have to be ready to do."

His wife did not seem to care much about Cromwell and King Charles First. Probably she had heard a good many times about her grandfather-in-law's ideas. But she too had something on her mind. To Debby's mother she said, "I feel like a different person! You know how terribly alarmed I've been about the Indians ever since we heard——"

Yes, Debby's mother knew, so her nod said.

"I've hardly had one good night's sleep since that dreadful news came in. I've had such nightmares! I'd wake up out of a sound sleep, sure that I heard the Indians yelling their war cry outside the house, sure that I smelled fire where they had put their torches up against the walls. And then I couldn't go back to sleep,

my heart was hammering so fast. I had to get up and
go to feel of the children to make sure they were all
right."

Yes, Debby's mother's grave face showed she knew
about those nightmares.

"But," their neighbor went on, "just now in the
State House yard, that fear left me. I never once
thought of it. And I don't feel it now. I thought of my
children's grandchildren, free to choose their own leaders."

"Yes, I too," said Debby's mother. "I stopped being
afraid. I thought only 'Now we are making a fresh
start. To try to do better. To make a government that
isn't for anything except to make its people safe, and
keep them free, and give them a chance to be happy!'
You know, you heard—'life, liberty and the pursuit
of happiness,' that's what our American government
is to be for!"

The two women kissed each other.

The neighbors went on into their house.

"Let's go sit down a minute under the pear tree,"
said Debby's mother. "I'm ready to drop."

The boys did drop. On the grass near their parents'
chairs.

"Whew!" they said, unbuttoning their collars and
taking off their coats.

"Say, Father," said the younger boy, "There was a
whole part in the middle that I can't remember at all.

I don't seem to have heard it even. I just heard the beginning and the end. What *was* the middle part?"

"It gave the reasons, fifteen years of reasons, for our wanting independence," said the father. "It's going to be printed in the newspapers. It'll be printed in lots of places. You can read it. Probably your schoolmaster will read it to you in school. But you know those reasons, anyhow, or most of them. We all do."

"I'm going to copy it off and learn it by heart," said the older boy, "every word of it."

Their father had set Debby down on her feet. She still clasped her doll.

"Well, Debby," he said, "you were a good little girl. You weren't the least bit of trouble."

Their mother said, "Do you know, Debby is the only one of us who hasn't said one word. Debby dear, what did you make of all that?"

"Oh, Mother, *she* couldn't understand anything! You liked the bells ringing, didn't you, Debby? That was the part *you* liked."

Debby looked around at her family circle, her blue eyes serious. "I've named my dolly," she told them, solemnly.

"Didn't she have any name?" asked one of her brothers, surprised.

"Only just 'Dolly'. And that's not a *real* name."

"Well, what did you name her?" asked the other boy, not much interested.

For a moment the little girl said nothing. Her earnest

little face grew pink with deep feeling. "It's a *beautiful* name," she said fervently.

They waited for her to tell them.

"What is it, dear?" asked her mother fondly.

"I've named her '*Sacred Honor*'," said Debby.

She was hurt by the long silence which followed. "Don't you *like* it?" she cried. "Don't you think it's a lovely name?"

Their father had to clear his throat. He laid his hand on his little daughter's head. "Yes, Debby dear, it's a very fine name. No dolly ever had a better."

PART II

THE CONSTITUTIONAL CONVENTION

1787

CHAPTER IX

ELEVEN YEARS LATER

ELEVEN YEARS CAN SEEM SHORT—OR A DAY CAN SEEM long. To a business man fifty-one years old, maybe his fortieth birthday does not seem so very long ago. Every morning since then, he has gone to his office. Nowadays the mirror tells him his hair is grayer; he can see that his children have grown taller. If he is lucky, his salary check is larger than it was. That is about all eleven years have brought him.

But when there is an earthquake with houses crashing down, it seems ever so long from morning to night. By sunset, everything is so different that a man can hardly remember what life was like when he got up in the morning.

For Debby's father and mother in Philadelphia the past eleven years had seemed just one earthquake after another. They could hardly think back to the time when their city had been part of a British Province, when sometimes they used to see Mr. Thomas Jefferson, or Mr. John Adams, and often old Dr. Franklin going back and forth along their streets.

Mr. Jefferson was now in Paris, Ambassador to France of their new country, the United States of America; Mr. John Adams was in London, Ambassador to England. You don't need to be told that he was getting a very, very cold shoulder from the fine people at the English Court. The King and his Ministers were still running the English government. They naturally hated to have any "American" Ambassador in England. And John Adams of all people! The King and his friends had always detested the very name of that Massachusetts man.

But Debby's family didn't worry too much about Mr. Adams in London. He could take care of himself. They remembered the time, eleven years before, when he'd been a delegate to the Continental Congress of 1776. He had looked then as if he thought that what happened to John Adams didn't amount to much, compared with what happened to his beloved country, the United States of America. So since somebody had to be the first American Ambassador at King George's court, and get cold-shouldered, it was a good idea to send Mr. John Adams of Massachusetts. For when anybody tried to be rude to him, he had a frosty, absent-minded look on his face that made people remember there are much more important things in the world than cross feelings about any one person.

Old Dr. Franklin was back in Philadelphia again, living in his own house, just down the street from Debby's home. He too had been across the ocean all this time, in France, representing the United States,

and was now more famous than ever. But also much
older. Eleven years is a long, long time when you're
past seventy to begin with. He was past eighty now,
and old, old, old. His legs that had been so lame, the
year when he had gone back and forth from the State
House, now wouldn't hold him up at all, even with a
cane. When he went away from home, he had to be
carried. Not even in a carriage. That would have been
too rough for the old doctor. Any jolt hurt him so
much he could hardly bear it. A sort of big box, with
a padded chair in it, was arranged for him, with long
poles on each side. Every morning his daughter helped
get her old father into this, some strong men put their
shoulders under leather straps, heaved up and, walking
slowly, carried the ancient philosopher in the first
sedan-chair Philadelphia had ever seen. The last one,
too.

But the fat old gentleman who suffered so much
pain and was likely to die any day was as cheerful as
ever, and still saw the funny side of things. When he
couldn't help it, the pain was so cutting, he groaned out
loud. But the next minute he'd be cracking a joke.

Somebody to be cheerful was very much needed just
then. For things looked pretty dismal. The Americans
had won the war against Great Britain, yes. But what
it had cost them!

The trouble was that they hadn't learned how to stick
together. Yet they couldn't get along if they didn't.

The trouble with the old way of sticking together,

which just hadn't worked at all, was that it had been
rushed through at the very time the Americans had
been at war with England. They couldn't possibly fight
the war, each State by itself. So in a great hurry, just
because they had to, they had made an agreement to
work together. This agreement was called the *Articles
of Confederation.*

It hadn't worked well during the war, and it was
hardly working at all now. Yet more than ever, the
States needed to agree with each other. Everywhere in
America, many people were scared to think how helpless
their own State would be, by itself, if it were attacked
by a big, rich European country with a fine army and
navy. And it was not only the great danger from outside. Inside the country there was already a lot of
jealousy between the different States. Some of them
were beginning to act as though there were no American
Confederation left at all, as if they were all separate
countries.

If they were separate countries, they would have dif-
ferences of opinion, and every time this happened they'd
go to war with each other, to get their own way. That
was the way the different European countries had always acted—fighting each other at the drop of a hat,
century after century. And look what they had lost in
money, deaths, poverty and misery!

There *must* be some way of getting together that
would work better than fighting each other. That's what
the Convention of 1787 in Philadelphia was to be for:
to invent a new set of rules (a Constitution) to make

that much-needed central government strong enough to do the things the States desperately needed and which they couldn't do, each one by itself.

Inside Debby's home there was not one new thing—except Debby. She was now a slim, long-legged fifteen-year-old girl—as tall as her mother. You'd never have known her for the chubby little chunk who had played in the sand-pile. It was a very happy home, full of love and fun; but everything except Debby was worn out and threadbare. Her mother's hair was gray, although she was only forty-six years old. Her father's was quite white at fifty. He had to have crutches to walk, because his left leg had been cut off. It had been frozen that dreadful winter the American army had spent at Valley Forge, with mighty little to eat, and thin ragged old coats and, even with deep snow on the ground, hardly any shoes at all.

The line of march of those American soldiers was red with blood from their bruised and bleeding feet. Yet their country was not so poor that it could not buy shoes for its own soldiers. The reason was a legal one. The Articles of Confederation—that first set of hastily invented rules—didn't provide any way for the Continental Congress to get taxes which would have brought in enough money from the States to buy new clothes and shoes and decent food for the American soldiers.

So Debby's father lost a leg for lack of the right kind of Constitution. He had a job now in the post office. It was work at a desk, work a veteran could do, even with one leg gone. The family had breakfast early, so that he would have time to hobble downtown on his crutches, for there was no money for a sedan-chair as for the great Dr. Franklin.

There was money, of course. He had a salary. But it was paid by the United States government. So his pay was in paper money. "Continental Currency" it was called, and that was worth just exactly nothing. Or almost. The Continental Congress hadn't had any legal power to make the States pay their fair share of the nation's expenses. Then, too, during the war there was so much confusion and uncertainty, and the States were so poor, that most of them paid very little. So the Continental Congress had to go on printing paper money. The more they printed, the less it would buy. People with things to sell were afraid it would be worth even less tomorrow than today. So they ran up the prices of food and clothing to be on the safe side.

If it hadn't been for the two boys, Debby's family would hardly have known how to manage at all. They were grown-up men of twenty-five and twenty-three now. The older one, like his father, had been in the American Army, and one winter had camped out in Chester County, not far from Philadelphia. There he had met a farmer's family, and—to make the story short—had gone back after the American victory which ended that long terrible war for Independence, and married the farmer's daughter. They had a little boy now. So Debby was "Aunt Deborah"—quite a change.

The farm was a fine one, on rich, deep, fertile soil. Americans were lucky in those hard days if somebody in the family lived on a farm! Once in so often the Chester County family would hitch up their two horses to the farm wagon, and drive in to visit the "old folks" in Philadelphia. They always brought presents from the farm. Sometimes it was a couple of fleeces from their sheep. Out of this wool Debby and her mother made homespun cloth for their menfolks' coats and breeches and their own winter dresses. Or they knitted stockings and coats and underwear and even winter nightgowns and nightcaps. Or they used that homespun thread for the endless darning and mending. Everything in the house was wearing out, rugs, wraps, underwear.

As for food, they used every inch of their back garden to grow vegetables. Years ago, there had been, so Debby's parents told her, a flower garden and a grass plot, where on summer evenings they often sat out under the pear tree. Now the pear tree stood in the middle of a small field, where peas and beans and squash and pumpkins and corn grew right up to the back door. Debby and her mother worked there, with her father, to raise food. Everybody on their street was raising food like this. The younger people couldn't remember when they didn't.

They went without a good many things—including anything new for the house. No, there *was* one new thing. A big framed picture of General George Washington. This hung over the mantelpiece. Debby couldn't remember when it had not hung there. But one day when she was cleaning the attic, her older brother was up with her. He found another framed picture, face down, under the eaves. Debby had never noticed it. He pulled it out, stood it up, wiped off some of the dust from it, and gazed at it a long time.

"Who is that?" asked Debby, leaning on a broom, her head tied up in a dusting cloth, looking over his shoulder. A man with a fat face like that shouldn't wear such a high collar."

Her brother was astonished. "Don't you *know?*" he cried out.

She looked again. "No. Should I?"

Her brother saw that she really didn't recognize the face. "Well, you *are* an American girl!" he exclaimed.

"That's King George III. It used to hang in our living room, just where General Washington's picture now is. Think of your not even remembering."

"Oh, I was only four years old," said Debby. "How could I?"

She went on sweeping, cautiously, not to raise too much dust. Her brother set the picture up and gazed at it. "It takes me back!" he murmured. "I remember so well the day when Mother took it down." To his sister he said, "Do you know, our brother told me that the last time his ship was in an English port, Bristol, I think it was, everybody there was gossiping about the King's going crazy. Really crazy, you know. Insane. People were saying he'd soon have to be locked up or put into a strait-jacket, to keep him from attacking the people around him."

Debby had no comment to make on this. She did not care a bit what happened to a king. Why should she? She was an American, and if there was one thing you could be sure of with any young American, it was that he wasn't interested in kings. Their parents sometimes talked about the King. When they did, they got angry. That was one of the queer ways older people had. They were always getting excited about something or other. For people of Debby's age, kings were already far in the past. They sounded like something in a book, like a "magician" or a "knight-at-arms." Something to read about, maybe, if you liked fancy stories. But no more.

Her brother was still gazing at the picture. He said

thoughtfully, "Maybe he was sort of crazy all the time? None of us ever thought of that."

Debby reached with her broom for a spider web on the slanting rafters.

"I suppose," meditated her brother, "that a person *is* crazy who gets so mad if every single person doesn't agree right off with every single thing he says."

Debby didn't pay enough attention even to hear this. It sounded like "history talk," to her, although it happened only eleven years ago.

But it did not seem to her the least bit like "history talk" when people discussed and argued and hoped about getting a Constitution that would be better than the agreement the States had hastily scrambled together in war times. Debby saw the need for that. Anybody with an eye in his head understood that if the States could really act together and support a central government, it would mean something. If they got some rules made about taxes paid to the government that would give her father his salary in good hard money—that would not be "history," that would be news.

They were all proud that Philadelphia was the place where this important Convention would be held. Yet her mother would not consider taking in one of the delegates as roomer or boarder. Other families around them did. There was an extra room in the house, the one the boys had had. But her mother shook her head.

"I don't mind living as poorly as we do," she said.

"I'm proud of the reason for it—that we are now free people in a free country, and I don't grudge what it cost. Not even your dear father's leg, not my gray hairs. But after all I'm a housekeeper. I can't bear to have a stranger from another State, where maybe they do have money to buy new things, come into this house and see everything patched and darned, even to the sheets on the bed. And have nothing to eat but fried Indian-corn mush and scrapple."

"Oh, I love fried mush and scrapple!" exclaimed Debby.

"You poor child! You can't even remember what a good meal is like—when we used to have roast leg of lamb, and fried chickens and jellies and custards whenever we wanted them. I'm not complaining! I count it a privilege to have given something up for independence. But all the same, I don't want strangers in here—maybe rich strangers—to see our rags.

"It's not our clothes I mind so much, although I sometimes wonder what my mother would have thought to see my petticoats, nothing but patches on patches. But housekeeping gear—she brought me up to keep a house in good condition. I haven't anything left to patch the towels *with!* And the covering on our chairs is so ragged that it won't take any more darning."

So one day in late May, 1787, when Debby went to the front door to answer a knock on it, and a strange man asked to see her mother about renting a room for the duration of the Constitutional Convention, Debby knew what her mother's answer would be.

But she went to get her and, because she was now considered a grownup, sat down in a corner of the living room to hear what was said. She let herself down light and easy, for that chair, like so much else in the house, was frail and old and one leg was cracked.

To her, the visitor looked like anybody else. He was a little younger than her father, but his hair was grizzled; he was dressed in gray woolen clothes, his shoes were of stout black leather with steel buckles, now rather dusty. He kept his left hand in his pocket.

"I've been trying everywhere, madam," he said, "to find a room within my means. My expenses here are paid in Continental money, of course. It's only fair to

let you know that, to begin with. And I haven't any
hard money of my own to spare. My business went
down a great deal during the war. I was sorry to have
to leave it now, just when it is beginning to look up a
little. At least, I hoped it was. A man hardly knows
how to run his business, with such uncertainty about
our money. I have a family, my wife and three boys.
And a baby girl born since the war. Like most people,
we barely make both ends meet. We live very plainly.
But my wife and I do not grudge the price. My wife
has been a patriot from the beginning."

He went on, "I need only a bed, breakfast and
supper. The main meal I plan to take with other
delegates at the Indian Queen Hotel. Several of the
wealthier delegates are living there—but that's beyond
my means—and the management of the hotel has arranged for a private dining room for those who wish to
eat together after sessions of the Convention. I believe
I can afford that."

He paused for the answer of Debby's mother. It
wasn't an answer yet. It was a question. "Were you—
did you serve in the war?" she asked.

"Yes, I enlisted among the first, I am proud to say.
That is how I lost this hand." He lifted his left arm
and showed a scarred stump.

"*Oh——!*" said Debby's mother softly. "In which
battle?" she asked respectfully.

"Not in battle at all," he said. "It was frozen, that
winter in Valley Forge. The army doctors had to cut it
off."

Debby's mother stood up and made the visitor a deep curtsey. "We will be glad to have you room with us," she said.

He stood up too, as men did when ladies were on their feet. Now Debby could see that, for all his simple clothes and quiet manner, he had a distinguished look about him.

"Thank you very much," he said with a bow. But he was still uneasy. "I hope the price——" he began. "I want to make it clear I have only Continental money——"

"We will be glad to accept any American money," said Debby's mother grandly, "till a new Constitution provides better." She said earnestly to him, "Sir, my husband lost his leg at Valley Forge. You are welcome in this American home."

CHAPTER X

HARD WORK AHEAD

DEBBY'S FATHER AGREED AT ONCE TO THE NEW PLAN.
He was especially pleased when he heard that the delegate had been in Valley Forge during that terrible winter which had cost him his leg. The two men did not
seem—at least to Debby and her mother—to talk together much about this, or about anything. But they
evidently enjoyed each other's company, nonetheless, in
the few hours they were together, smoking their pipes
in a comfortable, friendly silence, broken by an occa-
sional brief remark.

They were both tired when evening came; Debby's
father from his slow tiresome trip to and from his desk
at the post office, the delegate from the long steady
sessions of the Convention. The regular meetings began
at ten or eleven in the morning and lasted without any
recess till four or sometimes five in the afternoon.
And often enough, work on special committees had to be
done earlier or later than that. It made a long, hard
day.

Perhaps the delegate (Debby and her mother soon

spoke of him as "Our Delegate") was glad to have another tired man who expected nothing from him but
sociable silence while they waited for the evening meal
to be put on the table. Perhaps he was relieved to be
in a house where the family did not tease him to break
the promise, given by all the members of the Convention, not to tell anybody anything about whatever it
was they argued over, day after day.

The Continental Congress—the one which had put out
the Declaration of Independence when Debby had
been only four years old—had also agreed not to tell
outsiders about their debates. But that had been a very
different kind of meeting. They had constantly needed
news from the outside, from the different Colonies
which were, one by one, turning themselves into American States. Express riders had always, it seemed to
Philadelphia people, been coming and going to the
State House, their heavy, spurred, riding boots showing
the mud or snow or dust from far distant parts of the
country. Nobody knew what was in their mail bags, but
newspaper readers knew what was going on at Charles-
ton, or Hartford, or with the army. So with their newspapers and their gossip and with a public proclamation
from time to time, Philadelphia people had always been
able to piece together some notion of what the Continental Congress must be talking about inside the State
House.

But this Convention was different. The delegates
needed no more information from the outside than what
they had all brought with them to Philadelphia. They

knew—everybody did—that things were not going well,
that the country was in mortal danger. The American
States were falling apart—in spite of the wounds and
deaths and heart-breaking sorrow with which independence had been won. These sober-faced men from almost
all the States who now walked the streets of Philadelphia did not risk being hanged as traitors if they
failed. Yet if they failed, the Liberty Bell would have
rung in vain.

If they failed, their country would fail. The Revolutionary *War* was over and won. But not the Revolution.
There was no open army to fight. Now they had to
fight a harder battle, against a secret enemy, within
themselves, before the Revolution could be won. Now
they assembled not to fight a war against another
country, but to win a victory over that side of human
nature which makes everyone want his own way so
much that he comes to believe his way is the only right
way.

You've seen it happen when two toddlers want the
same apple. They grab and kick and scratch and—like as
not—tramp all over the apple as they fight each other,
so that what's left of it wouldn't be any good to either
of them. Looking on, it's easy to see that the sensible
idea is to cut it in two, so that each one can peaceably munch on his half. But you know how hard
it is to agree to a reasonable, sensible idea like that,
when you feel that you should have, by rights, all that
apple your own self.

The thirteen States, from New Hampshire to Georgia,

needed one another. They knew well enough they were not strong enough to stand alone. That is why they all (except Rhode Island, which was sulking) sent delegates to this Constitutional Convention. But could their delegates keep their heads and not get angry when they saw that no one of them could have *all* the apple?

That was the question before the delegates who, on a rainy day, May 25th, 1787, walked or rode to the State House, and met in the very same hall where the Declaration of Independence had been signed. All over America, people were hoping and praying that the delegates would succeed, because if they did, America could leap forward to be strong, prosperous, safe, happy.

All over Europe, kings and princes and prime ministers hoped they would fail, because that would prove what the rulers of those times wanted proved: that ordinary people aren't smart enough to run their own government, but must have a king or dictator to give them orders.

No wonder that Our Delegate looked very serious as he started off through the rain to the first meeting.

As far as Debby's family went, he walked away from the house into another world. He was an honorable man, and they were mannerly people who wouldn't dream of coaxing him to break his promise. So each morning when Debby handed her delegate his hat, held his overcoat for him to put on, and watched him walk away from the house, that was all. She knew nothing of what he did till he came back that afternoon, walking slowly, and glad to drop into a chair and silently smoke a pipe with her father.

But—did you ever happen to think of this?—history is like that magic carpet in the Arabian Nights' story. It can take you anywhere in the past.

Many, many years after this all-important Convention, when nearly every member had died, it was considered safe to publish the records of its work, day by day, speech by speech, debate by debate. Mr. James Madison of Virginia, one of the delegates, had taken down in a kind of shorthand what had happened, and fifty years after the end of the Convention, the American Congress in Washington, D. C. had this record printed in three volumes. These volumes probably stand somewhere on the shelves of your public library this minute. Anybody can read them—who knows enough to care to.

So it happens that we now don't need to stand with Debby in the front door of her home, watching the sober, gray-woolen-clad back of her delegate go down the street into an unknown world. With history to help us, we can walk right along beside him to the State House. There, armed soldiers paced up and down outside the building, outside the doors, and inside too, to make sure that nobody except the delegates came in. But no sentry can keep us out. With one of Madison's published reports, we can step along and see—what, at that time and for long years after, nobody else in Philadelphia, in America, in all the world, could see—just what was going on.

We'd see, first, the fine old hall, with white panelled walls, and tall windows on two sides (kept

In a chair on a low platform . . .
was General George Washington

closed no matter how hot the weather was, to prevent anybody from standing outside and hearing the talk inside.) In a chair on a low platform, in front of the delegates' seats, was General George Washington, who was President of this Convention. He was big-nosed, broad-shouldered, tall, ruddy-faced, just as he had been eleven years before. But then he was only a Virginia Colonel of Militia. Now he had been Commander in Chief of the American armies, all through those long, struggling, hoping, fearing, despairing and hoping again years of the War for Independence. Now he was one of the world's famous men.

In our country, he was famous because he had been the head general of our army and had, in the end, with the help of France, won our independence. What do you suppose he was famous for in England and in Europe? You'd never guess. Because when the war was over, he had thankfully taken off his uniform and gone back to farming. Most people outside America had expected him to use his fame and success and the fact that the army had the habit of taking orders from him, to make himself King of America.

Sounds funny to us, doesn't it? Imagine George Washington sitting on a throne with a crown on, and armed guards all around him. We can understand how good it felt when he could take off that stiff General's uniform and get into his old countrified clothes and decide which crop to put into which field on his farm.

But that was just what most people in Europe couldn't understand at all. And while some of them admired Washington for his astonishing (to them) idea of passing up the chance to grab and hold on to power, still they wondered whether he hadn't made a mistake. They thought that if he wasn't King, somebody would have to be. Perhaps someone not so good as Washington. There never had been a kingless nation (well, except a few tiny ones like Switzerland) so, if there never had been, that proved there couldn't be— they thought.

What such people outside of America were saying to themselves was something like this: "The Articles of Confederation had worked only after a poor fashion, even when those new American States simply had to stick together or get beaten in the war. Even then the American army hadn't been paid regularly (often hardly at all) nor well fed, nor decently clothed. And now that the war was over, the so-called central 'government' was cracking at the seams and breaking up into little pieces, into thirteen little pieces, not one of them amounting to anything. You just watch and see what a failure they'll make of this Constitutional Convention! Trying to patch up their old Confederation, are they? They won't make it any better. Can't be done— not without lords and dukes and a king and so forth and so on." That's what a lot of people outside of America thought and believed. And how they hoped they were right!

Just the opposite was hoped by the delegates as they gathered that first morning and looked up at George Washington in the President's chair.

How quiet he was. You'd never know from anything *he* did that he was one of the world's famous men. He never had been much of a talker, and now he had lost his own teeth and had artificial ones, carved out of ivory. They were the best any dentist in those days knew how to make; but they fitted his mouth so badly that talking was hard for him. But this was all right, as he was chairman of this meeting and the chairman is not supposed to say anything except to put the motion and keep the discussion in order.

Some of the delegates had been members of the Continental Congress which had voted the Declaration of Independence so they knew General Washington by sight. But for some of them this was the first time they had ever laid eyes on him—though his picture hung in nearly every American home. They gave this famous man a good long look, as you can imagine. And so can we, thanks to history. There he sat, tall, broad, blue-eyed, fifty-five years old, without much expression except a look on his face that showed he would never stop trying to do whatever ought to be done. He wasn't often lively or gay. But he never looked anxious or uncertain—although from history, which has let us read his letters to his friends, we know (what those delegates never knew) that he often was as worried as anybody else there, and as much afraid that they wouldn't make a go of it.

There was one other very famous man inside that hall, and we'd have looked at him after we'd taken a long look at George Washington, stately, composed, keeping a perfectly quiet face no matter how anxious he was over what was going on.

Down on the floor in one of the delegates' chairs sat Dr. Franklin. Sometimes he dozed off in an old man's cat-nap. But he never lost the thread of the discussions and was always ready to open his eyes to say something spicy, wise or funny. For he was naturally just as lively as George Washington was quiet. His broad, wrinkled old face was bright with interest in everything that went on, but it didn't show, any more than Washington's, what he was really feeling. For he too was terribly anxious for fear they might not make a go of putting together a set of rules that would really work.

For ten years he had been in France, representing America. He knew how great and rich and powerful people over there hoped and prayed that this Convention would turn out badly, and thus prove what they wanted proved, that everyday folks never know enough to run a country. Dr. Franklin knew too, how the everyday people of Europe, and the generous-hearted ones, whether they were ordinary or great folks, hoped and prayed for our success. All this weighed heavily on Dr. Franklin's old heart. He was well past eighty, and pretty sick too, and knew he hadn't long to live. But you'd never have guessed this from the bright face he showed at the meetings. His quick, alert eyes watched everything, sizing up each delegate as somebody who'd help or harm this great effort to step forward from the past and what governments always had done, to the future and what they might do.

We look back, through the door that History opens for us, and see the sick, anxious old man, easy and relaxed in his chair, his broad face so cheerful that it made people feel better just to see it. As for me, I take off my hat to Benjamin Franklin, and I hope you do, too.

CHAPTER XI

LET'S MAKE A
FRESH START

LET'S STAY ON HISTORY'S MAGIC CARPET FOR A WHILE
and watch—as Debby's family couldn't—how the delegates settled down to work during the first of their stay
at the State House. They were friendly and busy and
got along faster than you would expect. This was because the seven Virginia delegates had done a lot of
thinking in advance, had written out a plan for a new
Constitution, and had it all ready for discussion.

Governor Randolph of Virginia made a speech explaining the plan, and what was wrong with the old government. Just as if he had had the job of fixing up an old
bicycle or sewing-machine, he laid out all the parts
carefully, pointing to the broken and badly worn ones.

He drew special attention to the cogs and wheels
which had never been well designed and couldn't be expected ever to work well, because they never had.

It took him quite a while, and most of it was old
stuff to the delegates because they knew before they
got to Philadelphia, that there was plenty wrong with
the Articles of Confederation. But they listened with

patient attention, hour after hour. They knew that it was a life-or-death matter for their country. It was now or never for the States to find out how to stick together and make one nation, and if they didn't——! They hadn't come to that Constitutional Convention to be amused, but to save their country, so they listened carefully to every word.

But we don't need to. One of the advantages of History is that it lets you take short cuts to the most interesting places, instead of plodding, step by step, along the winding, tiresome road of things as they really happen.

What Governor Randolph said was about like this: He pointed out that under the Confederation the idea of the States was that they were independent (or "sovereign," as they called themselves). That meant that each State thought it could do just as it pleased. The agreement that joined them was that they would act together, yes, but only as much and when and as long as they pleased. This plan had not worked, as they all knew, and—so Governor Randolph said—it never would work because:

It didn't make them safe, since none of them could be *sure* of help from the others if it should be attacked by England or Spain or any other powerful foreign country.

And because,

There were lots of things needed in our nation, needed not by one but by all the States—such as keeping rivers open for ships, building canals (railroads were not dreamed of then, remember) for carrying goods and passengers, building good roads from State to State for getting the mail carried, a national army kept in good shape to help put down riots and rebellions too serious for the local State Militia to handle. These and other much-needed things would cost ever so much more than any one State had money for. But if they all put in their share, the money could easily be raised.

And because,

The central government ought to be able to crack down on any State which made laws hurting another—as New York was doing by charging a tariff on anything brought in for sale from New Jersey and Connecticut.

And so on and so forth. It was as plain as anything could be that those old parts of the Confederation couldn't be put together into any machine that would work. What they'd have to invent was a brand-new plan, with the States managing their own private affairs inside their own lines, but outside them, working with all the other States under rules they would all agree on. A central government would have to be set up, elected by the people of all the States. This central government would make laws to take care of things needed by the whole country—and it would need power enough to get those laws obeyed. AND, of course, since it couldn't get its work done without money, it would have to have the right to raise the money it needed by taxes. The old Confederation had had no way to pay its bills, except by promises that they would be paid sometime in the future, if somehow it could get hold of a little real money. That was the trouble with Continental money. That was why the Revolutionary Army had been badly paid, and poorly clothed. That was why Debby's father had lost his leg.

Whew! That was a pretty big mouthful for most of the delegates. Till then, they had thought of their States as independent countries, free at all times to decide what they would or wouldn't do. They didn't yet realize that nobody in the world can be free to do just what he pleases, any time he feels like it. If he does, he'll interfere with other people and they'll fight back. Well, maybe a single man, cast away on a desert island, without another soul there, could do what he liked any minute—except that one single man could not get much of anything done all by himself. He would need other people to work with, to get what he needed. And the minute you work with other people, you have to let them have their fair share.

But those American men at that Philadelphia meeting hadn't thought about all this. In those days, scarcely anybody had really understood that idea. Their legislatures had sent them to Philadelphia thinking that they could tighten up the bearings and put new oil and grease into the wheezy old Confederation machine and get it going. This plan for a new, superior, strong, national government went 'way beyond what they had expected.

Still, all of them had found out that you can't do

business—or run a government—you can't even pay
your household bills—with money that tomorrow will
buy less groceries, or overalls, or bricks and hardware
than it will today. Many of them had been almost
starved and frozen in the Revolutionary Army. They
knew Congress hadn't held back uniforms and rations
just to be mean. It didn't send food and shoes to the soldiers because it didn't have the money to buy them. Because even during the Revolutionary War, the States
never (even the best States) paid in their full share to
the general treasury. The men at that Philadelphia
meeting remembered the trail of blood left by cracked
bare feet on every winter march of the American Army.
So they decided that a national Congress would just
have to be given the right to tax—and to issue sound
money worth its face value.

But money wouldn't settle everything. There would
need to be general laws everybody had to follow
whether he liked it or not. You can see how they felt, if
you can imagine a basketball game where one team just
won't stop when the referee blows his whistle, but goes
on shooting goals. Without rules that everybody obeys,
you can't play a game, or run a business, or govern a
nation.

It went the same way with the other points. These
men had been around, and knew a lot about how to
run a business or a government, or they wouldn't have
been chosen as delegates. They might talk big about
every State having the right to do what it wanted,
any time. But they had sense enough to know that,

separately, not a single State would ever amount to much. But if the thirteen of them could agree to agree —they could certainly go places. It looked good.

Plenty of the delegates were worried about one part of the plan or another. They had fought so hard against the power of England to give them orders, they felt queer about the power that was to be given to the new central government by the new plan. "We'll have to look out, or first thing you know, we'll be ruled again by a king and prime ministers and dukes and whatnots."

"Well, we'll settle that later, when it comes to voting on details. Just now the question is, 'Shall we try to tinker up the old machine?' "

"No, that's evidently a waste of time. It'll never run."

"Shall we start fresh, and invent a new government with a new Constitution?"

The vote went, "Yes, we will! There's nothing else to do."

All this while Debby's family were bursting with curiosity. They never asked direct questions. But they did look hard at their delegate when he came for supper, and try to guess by his manner how Convention business was going. Pretty well, they thought—at least as well as could be expected. Some nights he seemed tuckered out from listening to long speeches and he always looked serious from carrying a great responsibility, but at least for some weeks he seemed quite easy in his mind. His appetite was good. He told them about his wife, and his little red-haired, post-war daughter, "The first American-born in our home," as he said. He was interested in the garden.

"We'll have peas for supper before long," said Debby's mother, "and maybe the Indian corn will be ripe before you go home." Then she bit her lips and blushed, for fear he might think she was trying to draw from him an opinion as to how long the Convention would last. It was really hard *always* to remember that he had promised not to tell anybody a single thing about what he did all day.

Debby thought it was nonsense. "What's the use of being so secret?" she asked.

Her father thought a while, then finally answered. "I suppose the idea of this Convention is to talk over all the possible plans for government and finally pick out the one that promises best. Now some men seem to want to know right away what to do. But of course as a matter of fact nobody *is* smart enough to know without thinking. They are here to put their heads together and talk reasonably and listen to reason. It might be easier for them to be convinced by somebody else's good ideas and change their own, if people in general didn't know how they voted at first. But that is only my guess. I really don't know."

He never knew. He died an old man without knowing. They none of them knew anything. All they could do was to have as good breakfasts and suppers as they could for their delegate, and make up his bed carefully with the least patched of the sheets—and watch his face to see whether he looked cheerful or not.

CHAPTER XII

ROSES FOR DEBBY

ALL THROUGH THOSE EARLY WEEKS DEBBY'S DELEGATE looked calm and untroubled in spite of his load of responsibility . . . as if he felt that somehow or other everything would work out all right. Once he even said so. Debby's father had been telling him that it was only because of the hard times that they had to use all their back yard to grow food. He said that before the war they had had a pleasant strip of grass near the house, and some benches under the pear tree where they often sat, of a summer evening.

"You will again," said the delegate heartily. "When our Convention has finished its labor, our nation's affairs will be in order as they have never been before. Our debts will be paid. A good taxation system will bring in a reasonable revenue to our national government. We can expect our commerce to grow greatly. Our shipping will need to grow as much. Your son will be a ship's captain. Your salary, sir, will be paid in gold coins, if you would like it so. And Miss Debby here can have India-lawn dresses, all printed over with posies."

That was good news.

But about the middle of June, their guest stopped being cheerful. He came back to the house dragging his feet. He was always mannerly and never gruff, but he grew more and more silent. He was thinking hard about something. It was something so troubling, if they could judge from his darkened face, that he hardly heard what they said to him, hardly saw what was around him in the house, in the vegetable garden, on his plate.

His appetite left him, too. It was the time of year when, in the Philadelphia climate, the strawberries are ripe, the green peas are meltingly delicious, the asparagus and the rhubarb are still tender and savory. The future of the country depended on what was done by the Constitutional Convention. The family on the fine farm in Chester County felt, as everybody else did, that they wanted to do their share to honor a delegate to the meeting from which so much was hoped by the whole nation, so they sent or brought in young broilers, fresh eggs, rashers of bacon, hams, a guinea hen once in a while. Deborah had never eaten so well in her life. But their guest picked forlornly at this delicious food, "like a sick child," mourned Debby's mother. He ate a little, and sat, his knife and fork in his hand, staring at nothing.

They were all deeply troubled. For there could be no reason for his low spirits except that the Convention was not going well.

Towards the end of June, their delegate addressed himself to Debby's mother one evening. "Madam," he said, "I trust what I am about to ask will not seem improper to you. My sleeping is poor these nights. In fact I am hardly sleeping at all. I have thought that perhaps if I could, sometimes, without disturbing your household, arise and walk up and down the path in your garden it might allay my restlessness."

Debby's mother begged him to do anything that might be of help to him.

Debby's father said, after hesitating a little, "Sir, my nights, too, are not good. Would it be presuming if sometimes I joined you there?"

The delegate took his host's hand in his. "It will comfort me, my friend, to have a veteran from Valley Forge with me." He said this in a voice that trembled a little.

So, during the hot first part of July, Debby and her mother often heard the stairs creak as their guest went down in his stocking feet. He paused a moment silently at the door of the downstairs bedroom where Debby's father slept, and then went on to sit on the threshold of the back door to put his shoes on. Then, often, there was the familiar thump of the crutch in the hall— and out into the darkness went the two veterans to pace slowly up and down the garden path on the soft open ground, between the rows of Indian corn, growing taller by the hour, it seemed, in the hot darkness.

Although Debby's mother didn't walk the floor those nights, she too did not sleep well. She lay in her bed,

her eyes wide open in the blackness, her heart heavy, her mind full of fears. She had a cousin about her age whose husband worked as clerk in the State House, but not for the Convention. Mr. James Madison of Virginia and an official Secretary took notes there of what went on. But there were other offices in the building, where clerks copied out documents, and made up accounts for the State of Pennsylvania. Sometimes, when they couldn't keep up with this desk work, they went back to their desks in the evening to finish it.

Debby's mother had never told her cousin anything about the sleepless night wanderings of their delegate. She did not tell anybody, and made Debby promise not to mention it. "It might make people fear things are not going well with the making of the new Constitution," she said. "Since we have a delegate in our house, we must take our share of his promise of not letting people know anything about their proceedings."

But she herself found it hard not to show her alarm at something her cousin told her, about this time. "Do you suppose," said her cousin, "that they are having trouble getting together on the Constitution in the Convention?"

"What makes you think that?" asked Debby's mother quickly, looking and feeling as anxious as she had been when her husband was in the Continental Army, half starved, half frozen, without enough powder and shot for his musket.

Her cousin went on, "Well, I wouldn't speak of it to anybody but you, but this is what my husband told me. Last night he was working at his desk in the State House, and happening to look out of the window, saw that somebody was inside the walls of the Yard. You know nobody is supposed to go in there now, during the time the Convention is meeting. The armed sentries have orders to keep everybody out. My husband went down to call one of the sentries. But he didn't. For who do you suppose it was, walking up and down there in the twilight? General Washington! General George Washington. All by himself. Walking up and down, up and down the path, his hands behind his back. All alone. It was getting darker. He didn't notice. He just walked up and down, up and down——"

Debby's mother could not speak. She gazed silently at her cousin as she went on, in a lower voice that was not very steady, that sounded as though she had a lump in her throat, "It made me think of when my mother died. I walked up and down like that all night long. It was after she was so far gone she didn't recognize any of us. There was nothing we could do for her by staying in her room. I couldn't bear to sit there and watch her die. I went out of the house into the road—we lived in the country then—and walked up and down all night. Till I saw the curtains drawn—and knew that my mother was dead."

The two American women gazed palely at each other, in heartbroken alarm. Was their country dying?

But then—oh, what a relief! the delegate actually cleaned up his plate at supper, and told them how much he had enjoyed the tender young string beans. Their spirits soared. Things must be going more smoothly at the Constitutional Convention.

Their spirits soared higher still on the 13th when he came into the house, a broad smile on his face, bringing a bouquet of roses for the table. He said he had overheard them remarking that July 13 was Debby's birthday.

They were happy that evening, although the Philadelphia family had no idea what had been the matter. They were proud too, over a compliment to their State paid by their guest as he smoked his pipe with Debby's father.

"Very fine men you have in Pennsylvania," he said. "You have reason to be proud of them."

Debby's mother answered, "Yes, Dr. Franklin is indeed a great sage and a famous philosopher."

"I am sure he is," said their guest, "but I was speaking of your Mr. Wilson." He drew a long pull on his pipe, took it out of his mouth, looked up at the ceiling as though he were trying to think of the right words, and said warmly and emphatically, "Mr. Wilson is an honor to the human race."

Debby stared, not knowing the name. Her mother quickly gave her a Philadelphia-ish explanation, "He's a cousin of Molly Cutler's mother."

And that was all Debby knew—till fifty years later.

But *we* can know. We can know, now this minute, what Debby did not know till she was an old woman— what the delegate had been through that summer day of July 13, when she was sixteen years old. If we step on History's magic carpet, it will whisk us back to that big hot room, with those heated men angrily quarreling.

But although we can know, through Mr. Madison's report of the meetings, exactly what happened to the Congress and the delegates on that July 13, we can't understand why it made the delegate feel like giving somebody a bouquet of roses, unless we go back to earlier meetings.

The first days had been full of pleasant, vague good will. "The Virginia plan" had been carefully invented with detailed clauses and sub-headings all thought out to take care of anything that might happen to a government, with judges and courts, and representatives in a legislature—everything provided for. The other delegates hadn't anything prepared, and for the first weeks they all sailed forward on general ideas.

Then they had run aground on a rock. On a concrete fact, on the fact that some States were large and had lots of people in them. And other States were small. Smashingly, everything had come to a halt. They were hung up on a difference of opinion which just couldn't ever—so far as they could see—be settled, because the fact would never change. There would always be large States and small ones. And people had grown so used to the ideas of States that it seemed against nature to admit that some of them were less important than others. How could any government be invented which would be fair both to the small States, such as Delaware and New Jersey, and to the big States, such as Massachusetts and Pennsylvania?

There was to be a national legislature. Of course. No argument. For many years they had all grown used to that way of government in their own States. Well, then, should the national law-makers be elected by the State legislatures? A few delegates thought so, but they didn't put up much of a fight. It was settled that the people should vote directly for one part of the national legislature (the one we now call the House of Representatives).

How many of these representatives should each State send? That was a hard question. If every forty thousand people elected one representative, that would mean only one or two apiece for each of the smaller States. They didn't like the idea. Under that plan a couple of the bigger States could out-vote all the smaller ones. Delaware and New Jersey representatives might as well stay home for all the influence they would have.

The big States came right back with the question, "Is it fairer to vote the way we now do in the Continental Congress—and right here in the Convention—one vote to each State, large or small? That means that a few people in seven small or medium States can give order to a lot more people in the other six States."

In general, as far as the logic of the argument went, the large States had the best of it, and the little States shouted and screamed and threatened that if they couldn't have their way, they'd go back home. But in this matter such a threat was tragically serious. For it would be very dangerous to have some of the States standing out from the Union. Dangerous to the solitary State, and even more dangerous to the whole country.

The danger of a failure to get all the States into one nation was, finally, brought out in red-hot, angry words, when one of the delegates from Delaware said furiously that his State would never, never submit to the larger ones. Had they fought and suffered in the war for Independence to fall under the tyranny of their neighbors, worse than that of King George III? They had not. He was shouting rather than speaking, he was so excited, and he went on with the threat that if Delaware did stay out of the Union, she might make a bargain with a foreign country, become part of some nation from across the Atlantic, which would give her a better deal than her fellow-Americans.

In that company of men who had fought so wildly to get out of the power of a nation from across the Atlantic, this threat of having such a nation established in their midst was as horrifying as if, in the midst of their human voices discussing ways and means, a tiger had suddenly let out a snarl. (That was the time when Debby's delegate didn't notice what was on his plate for supper, and walked desperately up and down the garden path, although it rained most of the night.)

Well, they kept at it hammer and tongs for days. Something had to be done.

And something was done.

We Americans must never forget that in every crisis, something was done. They did not break up the Convention, and give up trying. It is to the eternal glory of the Constitutional Convention that although all the members wanted their own way, they wanted still more to set up the best possible government for their country.

What they did now was to appoint a committee, one member from each State to see if they couldn't find *some* sort of a plan everyone could agree to. Just after the fourth of July, this committee brought in its report: In the House of Representatives there should be one representative for every forty thousand people . . . that gave the larger States the most power there. But in the

National Senate, every State should have an equal vote, the small States just the same as the big ones.

This is called *"The Federal Compromise."* To our day, now, this is the way we run our government in Washington.

Nobody was altogether satisfied with it . . . it was like cutting the apple up and giving everyone a slice. But at first, at least, it looked as if it had broken a path through the solid wall that seemed to shut them away from progress, toward a union everyone could agree to.

Those were the days when Debby's representative began to feel better, and stopped walking in the garden most of the night. Maybe the new plan wasn't the very best one imaginable, but it might work, if everyone gave it a fair chance.

But just then something happened that almost broke his heart. One morning a delegate got up and said it was moonshine and foolishness to pretend that all questions ought to be settled by counting noses. "Money is power," he said. "Wealth ought to count just as much as the number of voters in a government which like all governments, really is formed for the protection of property . . . since government is supported by property."

Another delegate pointed out that a lot of poor people were moving over the mountains into western lands. Before long there might be more votes there than in the rich, old, settled, original thirteen States along the sea coast. *That* couldn't be allowed!

And then, before anyone knew just what was happening, it was voted that for all new States, representation in Congress should be figured partly on the number of voters and partly on *how much money they represented.*

Those were bad days and nights for our delegate. At first he was so discouraged that he didn't even have strength enough to get up and walk in the garden. He just lay awake in his bed and worried. Protection of property was all right. No one would work hard and be thrifty unless the law protected his savings. And it was true enough that a rich man, just because he was rich and could hire and fire men working for him, had always more power than a poor man. But that didn't

prove that the law ought to be rigged to give him more
power still. Nor that he was any better as a citizen than
an honest, brainy man who hadn't so much money.

It got so bad that one night (it was the night of July
12th, just before Debby's birthday) the delegate dragged
himself out of bed again. Step by step, to and fro on
the garden path he walked, trying to figure it out. Was
it all worth while, he asked himself, as he looked
around him in the starlight at the humble vegetable
garden and the crippled man beside him. Was it to set
money ahead of human beings, that this man lost his
leg? Had he been fighting in the American Army, not
for his country as he thought, but to make money powerful? Did the surgeon at Valley Forge cut off this hand
of mine to give more power to a rich man than to a
poor one? Was it just to safeguard money that in the
Declaration of Independence we Americans all pledged
—through our representatives—"our lives, our fortunes
and our sacred honor?" "Honor" is a great word, he
thought, plodding to and fro on the earth of that path.
Did I then promise by my sacred honor that I would do
my best to keep rich men in power in our government?

He had always thought and felt deeply about his
country and her welfare, but he was not much of a public speaker himself. He did not know what he could say,
he a plain citizen, in answer to these orators who had
all the words at their tongues' ends. Perhaps other
delegates agreed with their idea. They seemed to. Nobody protested. Perhaps he was the only person in the

Convention who did not like this pulling off your hat to money, rather than to character, honesty and good sense. His fellow-delegates seemed by their silence to take it for granted that if a man had money, it proved he had more character and honesty and good-will and intelligence than a man who hadn't. He knew well enough that this was not true. But if all the others there thought so——

Next morning he was worn after that sleepless night. He ate his hominy and bacon and corn bread and molasses for breakfast, his mind full of anxiety. Very dimly he heard somebody at the table say that this was the birthday of the young daughter of his hosts. But this news went in one ear and out the other, so filled was his mind with despondent ideas.

He walked to the State House and slumped into his chair. Then things began to happen. First Mr. Randolph, a rich man from Virginia, the Governor of that State, made a motion. And would you believe it? He moved to strike out the word "wealth" in the rules for giving representatives to new States.

Mr. Wilson of Pennsylvania stood up to speak next. Our delegate was worried. Wilson was a bright man, one of the clearest thinkers in the Convention. But he was a lawyer, and lawyers are likely to think a good deal about taking care of their rich clients. After a few words our delegate stopped worrying.

It was a long, brilliant speech. But he never forgot any of it. What it amounted to in plain words was this: "All men wherever they live have equal rights. We

need not be troubled by the fear that some day the
"Interior Country" might have more votes than the old
States. If they come to have the most votes, then they
will deserve to run the government. We must not forget
that England tried to keep America from growing too
strong . . . and as a result the British forced us to
fight and to win our freedom. We of the old States
must not make the same mistake with our western
settlers. And as for the argument that "wealth must
rule"—here his voice rang out clear and strong—he
said he didn't believe a word of it. "Property is NOT
the chief object of government and society," he said in
so many words. "Society's chief and most noble purpose is the cultivation of the human mind." Therefore
he hoped others would join him in supporting Mr.
Randolph's motion.

Our delegate had been thirstily drinking in every one
of these splendid words. It seemed too good to be
true that Mr. Wilson, the great Pennsylvanian lawyer,
so respected for his brains and his education was talking like—yes, that was it—Mr. Wilson was making
them all remember what Thomas Jefferson had written . . . "We hold these truths to be self-evident."

He himself was ready to yell out his vote against
counting wealth higher than human values. But would
any other delegate vote that way, he wondered? They
had sat so silent when Gouverneur Morris had said
that "savages might be interested in life and liberty, but
for civilized people, property is the main object of
Society" . . . or when Mr. Rutledge and others had

repeated that "Government is for the purpose of making money secure."

General Washington quietly put the question, "All in favor of Mr. Randolph's motion will say 'Aye.'" Our delegate had been sitting on the edge of his chair, waiting for that question. One thing was sure. Whether there was a single other vote for the motion to strike out the word "wealth", there would be a loud one from him. His "aye" was going to be a shout.

And what do you think happened? His shouted "aye" was drowned out in a storm of everybody's "ayes." Every State represented, except one, voted to leave out the word "wealth." During all the meetings of the Convention, there was hardly another vote on which they were so united. In their hearts, they had *all* been thinking just what our delegate thought. Even those who had spoken in favor of counting wealth as being as important as human beings, had been carried along. Mr. Wilson had called out to them to climb up and stand where the air was fresh and free—and how they had all followed him!

That afternoon when his usual late-afternoon meal with the other members of the Convention was finished, our delegate felt so happy, so relieved, so made over, that he couldn't just walk back into the house and sit down in a chair. He was full of new hope and life! He'd have to use up some before he could be quiet. Strange to be restless now because he was happy! It felt fine.

He struck out at random, up one street and down another, wherever his feet took him. "——'property is

not'," he said aloud, quoting from Mr. Wilson's
speech, " 'the sole or primary object of Government
and Society'."

He walked faster, made a wide sweep with his arm.
"The most noble object is the cultivation and improvement of the human mind——" he said earnestly to a
sycamore tree. "We are founding our country's government not to give men a chance to get rich, but to live,
be free, find out *how to be happy.*"

" 'Life, liberty and the pursuit of happiness'," he exclaimed to the nearest lamppost. He forgot his usual
care to keep the ugly scarred stump of his left arm out
of sight in his pocket. He was proud of it and what it
meant, for it *had* been worthwhile, after all, to have
fought the war for Independence.

People glanced back at him as they passed—a sober,
middle-aged, quietly dressed man, yet talking to himself
as he went along the street, his face shining with joy.

Presently his eyes told his brain that something
bright-colored was in front of him. He slowed down
his swinging pace. What was it? Flowers. Summer
roses. He had come into the flower-market. Well, that
was appropriate. He felt as though flowers had sprung
up all along his path.

As he looked, he remembered dimly—didn't somebody
speak of today's being a birthday? Whose could it be?
Not one of his children. Oh, yes, the young girl at his
boarding house. "Give me that bunch of roses, will you
please?" he said to the woman at the stand, and reached
into his coat for his pocketbook.

CHAPTER XIII

ANOTHER HILL
TO CLIMB

HAVE YOU EVER BEEN ON AN ALL-DAY SCOUTING HIKE, scrambling through scratchy brambles and over stones that hurt your feet, hot, out-of-breath, leg-weary? How good it feels about three o'clock in the afternoon, when the trail levels off. You're sure you've done the worst of it. Now, you think, it'll be easy to stick it out to the end. And then through a gap in the trees you see that ahead of you is a real mountain trail, winding up over rocks, rough, and steep, steep, steep!

The members of the Constitutional Convention must have felt like that a few days later, on July sixteenth. This time it wasn't the question of a State's having more votes if it had more money. Mr. Wilson had killed that idea for good and all. It was the old argument over one-vote-to-each-State in the Senate. Virginia, Pennsylvania and South Carolina made one last try to upset that. They couldn't quite do it, so the *Federal Compromise* still stood, but when the rumpus was over that part of the plan had a majority of only a single vote. Everybody thought in discouragement, "Oh, what's the use? We'll never get our plan adopted by the States, if we are so divided ourselves about it."

Remember that by their voting these delegates had no power to bind anyone except each other. Suppose you and some of your friends were working on a committee to draw up rules for your school athletic club . . . you would discuss and vote just as they did, until you had agreed on the best set of rules you could think of. But your set would be only suggestions and no one would have to follow the rules you planned unless the whole club voted to accept them. That was the way with the Convention. The States had the final say-so. When the Constitution was finished, it had to be voted on by conventions in each of the thirteen States. If nine of these States liked it, the new government was to start, in the hope that the other four would come in later. Unless nine States were willing to try it, nothing would happen . . . except to drop the Constitution into the waste-paper basket and try to forget about it.

No wonder they were dismal that day when they found they were still almost half-and-half divided on one of their most important ideas. After working all summer, talking, thinking, explaining, if they hadn't got together any closer than that, what chance would their Constitution stand in the State conventions? Not much, they thought. We might as well give up and go home, many of them thought. A few of them said just that, out loud.

What we must never forget is that they didn't go home. They weren't the sort to quit. Like the Scout troop at the foot of the steep hill, they wiped the perspiration out of their eyes, tightened their belts and said to one another, "Come on, let's go!" And the first thing they knew, they were over the hump.

It happened this way. Next morning, before time for the meeting to begin, delegates from the big States came to the Assembly Hall and sat around the President's table to talk things over. They spoke their minds right out. This idea of one vote in the senate to each State, no matter how small—it's not fair, they said. Nothing could make them think differently. But after all it had been voted. Mr. Rutledge said something like this: "Even though we can't do what we think best, we ought to stick around and do the best we can. That's what we're here for." He said what most of them were thinking.

By this time, a good many delegates from the smaller States had come into the hall and were standing near the table and listening to Rutledge and the others.

"Why, these big boys are square shooters," they thought. "They aren't planning to gang up on us and push us around. And they're right about not quitting. We're here to do the best we can, even if our best isn't perfect. They say they don't like everything in the proposed Constitution. Well, *we* don't either! But if we work all together and keep at it, we can certainly turn in a plan of Government a lot better than the Articles of Confederation. We've got to."

From that day on, the going was better. I don't mean that it was all downhill on a gentle grade. There were plenty of rough spots, plenty of disagreements, plenty of sharp words during debate . . . but no one doubted any longer that some sort of a Constitution was going to be worked out.

What did they disagree about? About almost every idea that came up. For one thing, about having a president. Everyone knew that someone has to be on the job all the time to see that laws are carried out, to make sure that money is honestly and carefully spent . . . and in general to act as the chief and head of our government. But would it be wise to trust all that power to one man? Maybe a committee of three would be safer. Do you wonder what ever put such a crazy suggestion into their heads? Can you think what they meant by "safer"?

The same old fear was worrying them. A single president might sooner or later get all the power into his own hands and make himself King. Three men could watch one another. Some of the delegates said foolish things about Caesar and Oliver Cromwell, and the "Tyrants of ancient Greece," but fortunately most of the members of the Convention kept their wits about them. They pointed out that a board of three governors would be continually passing the buck, round and round. Nothing would ever get decided. A single boss can make up his mind and stick to it. So we got a single president, and now after 160 years we still live under a republic, not a despotism.

Do you think the delegates were silly to worry so much about something that was never going to happen? Think a minute. It could have happened. It actually did happen, not so long ago in Italy and Germany. And at all events, even when they had their worst jitters about the danger of somehow getting an emperor or a king or a dictator slid over on them, the Convention members were nothing to the people back in their home States, who were always looking under their beds and inside their closets, to make sure a king was not hiding there. The delegates kept getting letters from their fellow-citizens telling them they must *not* provide for a king in the Constitution. And one time, the rumor got around that the Convention was planning to bring over as King of America, one of the sons of King George Third. George Third's son, of all people! The delegates were anxious and tired and worried, but they got one good laugh out of that.

There were plenty of other questions still to be worked out. Who was to elect this president? Should he be elected by Congress? Or by the State Legislatures? Or by all the citizens in a general election? The Convention had to decide which they would choose.

And law courts—some rules had to be made about those. Each State had its law courts. But how about disputes growing out of the national laws Congress was going to make? Shouldn't there be some sort of national law court, to settle these? The new Constitution did provide for such a national law court and this was the start of our Supreme Court.

After this, the question of treaties with foreign countries came up. Who would have the power to make those? And tax-money? How much of the money raised by taxes should be granted to the central government? How much should be left to the States? And so on and so on. It would be foolish to try to set down here all the questions and how each one was settled. You can find that in any book on Civics.

Nobody needs to try to learn a big lot of facts he can easily find in books. That would be like trying to learn the dictionary by heart. It's enough if you know how to look up the spelling or meaning of any word. The same thing is true about the Constitution. You couldn't possibly remember all its sub-divisions and clauses.

But there is one thing we all ought to know and never to forget—that is, the big, basic idea at the bottom of all the facts in our Constitution. There is just one. Our whole national government rests on it. It's easy enough to learn by heart for there are only three words to it—"checks and balances."

This is what it means. Nearly every human being likes to be the one who tells other people what to do. In planning for any group of people who are going to work together—a big national government, or a church sewing circle, or an athletic association, or a student council—rules or laws must be provided to keep one or a few members from bossing the others, or from running a part of the work just as he pleases. Here's one example that we all know: In an athletic association, the treasurer takes in the money. It won't do not to provide some "check" on him. He must not be left to be boss of the finances, all by himself. Generally the rule is that he must show his accounts to the other officers of the association, let them know how much money there is in the treasury, and tell them just what's been done with the money he has spent. The right of the other officers to know about the work of the treasurer, is the "check" on him which keeps things in "balance."

If you did not do that, your club might get along all right as long as you always had a perfectly honest treasurer. But suppose, some year, you happened to elect a pretty good fellow, a pleasant likeable boy, but one of those people who just can't keep money from running through his fingers. First thing you'd know, he'd have spent all the money in your treasury and you wouldn't have a thing to show for it. He needs—nearly all of us need—a "check" to keep us from doing things too much according to our fancy.

Our American public schools are based on the same idea of "checks and balances." Nearly everything in the United States of America is. We're so used to it, we don't often think of it. But the minute you do think, you see the point. For instance, the classroom teacher marks the mid-term examination papers and the daily recitations. Of course. He (or she) is the one to decide how good a student's work is. And usually that is the way to manage. But suppose a teacher is terribly worried about something at home—a sick mother, or the loss of a lot of money. His mind might not be entirely on those examination papers. He might flunk a student who hadn't done too badly. There must be some way provided for a "check". The usual thing is to have a principal of the school, to whom the student and his parents can go with the examination marks they don't think fair. By the usual rules, the principal is given the right—if the student and his folks ask him—to look over that examination paper and see what he thinks about the mark. In law this would be called an "appeal to a higher court."

The Founding Fathers knew that in the Constitution they were inventing, they'd have to make sure that no group of officials, and no single person, can run things too much his own way. That's the chief reason for having both a Senate and a House of Representatives. Each acts as a "check" to the other, each helps balance up the power given by the country.

What every American should always remember is not the long list of facts about what was voted at the Constitutional Convention, but the principle of checks and balances, for that is what we've always tried to keep alive and strong in our country. It has some disadvantages. It slows things up. It's apt to cause a tremendous amount of arguing and discussion. But we think discussion about our government is a good thing. In the long run we think that our principle is what has kept any one person, or any one set of people, from bossing the rest of us around too much. Our votes on election day are the final decisive "check."

Now you can see why the delegates to the Constitutional Convention had to work so hard. It wasn't enough to believe that a system of checks and balances is the right one. They had to invent rules that would make the principle apply in every single place in our government. Every sentence they wrote had to be closely studied, not only by itself but compared with other items already agreed to. Who must do what? And where must he stop? It all had to be thought out, so that someone would handle each one of the many, many pieces of business that altogether make up good government. And yet there must be no chance left for one officer to say to another, "You keep out of this. . . . This is my business."

Oh, what a relief it was when, towards the hot end of that hot July, the Convention voted to take a recess! This was the very first break in their every-single-day, all-day-long work since they arrived in Philadelphia. The recess was to last for ten days, while a special committee studied and considered in even greater detail every word of that Constitution. They were to make sure that no part of it contradicted any other part, and that every sentence of it would stand up in law courts when—perhaps in the future—clever lawyers might try to make a sentence mean what the men who wrote it didn't intend it to mean.

Our delegate was mighty glad he was not a lawyer who might have been put on this special committee. He wanted a rest! He really was almost worn out! If we find it hard just to read about the work they did, you can imagine how tired it made them to do it!

At first he couldn't think how he would like to spend that vacation. His home was too far away to go back to it. But then he had an idea.

CHAPTER XIV

THREE OLD SOLDIERS

WHEN DEBBY'S FATHER HEARD WHAT THE IDEA was, and that he was a part of it, he joyfully smacked one hand into the other. Yes, indeed, he would go with the delegate! What's more, he would provide transportation. His son, the farmer, had a steady old horse and small chaise, just big enough for two, and he would be glad to let them use it for a couple of days.

To Debby's mother he explained, "We think we'd like to make a visit to Valley Forge." He needed to say no more. His wife's face softened, darkened, melted. "Don't cry, dear," he said. "It's all in the past."

"It's not in the past to *me*," she said, blowing her nose, and wiping her eyes. "I never hand your crutches to you without raging that you went through all that horror, just because our Articles of Confederation didn't give our Congress power enough to tax the States to get money for the army. When I hear sometimes a young person say that 'taxation is a tiresome subject'——!" She drew a long breath and went on, "Women's memories are longer than men's! I can't forget the dreadful way we all learned what taxes can mean for human beings."

Then, thoughtfully, "I'm glad you're going back there. I hear it's all grown up to green things, bushes and grass, so a person, to look at it, would never know the misery of that winter's camp."

"Nature's memory is short—like men's," said her husband.

"I'm glad you have somebody to go with, too," she said. "Another man who'll know how you are feeling. He won't get as excited as I would. I never want to look at that place."

The chaise and the stout old farm horse stood at the door. Debby and her mother trotted to and fro with extra wraps and stockings, and the big lunch basket, and some towels in case the country inn shouldn't be really clean, and a pillow——

"There, there," said Our Delegate, laughing. "We're not going to drive to Georgia. Only to Valley Forge We'll be back by tomorrow evening. Even if it should rain. . . .!"

He helped Debby's father in, settled his crutches beside him, climbed in on the other side, took off his cocked hat and waved it to Debby and her mother. Then he picked up the reins, clucked to the horse, and the chaise jogged away down the street.

"How cheerful they both looked," said Debby wonderingly. How could people so very old—her father was fifty-five and Our Delegate must be in his forties—who

had been through such terrible things, look like two boys
going off fishing together?

It was dusk the next day when the chaise jogged
back. The weather had been fair. No rain. Probably
everything had gone along all right.

But it was not "all right" that was written on the
faces of the two men. It was "Hallelujah!"

"*You* tell them," said Debby's father after they had
got themselves into the house and were sitting together
in the living room. So the delegate did, "We found it all
gone back to a state of Nature," he said, "grass growing

thickly where our tents had stood, young trees starting up where the earthworks had been. It made us feel very sober to stand there and look back. And remember.

"We found a place to eat lunch. A corner of what had been the drill ground. An old tree had fallen across it, to make a bench and a table. We sat there, opening your lunch basket, when we saw someone walking down the drill ground towards where we were. We were not surprised. We thought probably some other old soldier with a day or so off from work had had the same idea we had—to go back and see how it looked. We'd be sure to see anybody who did, because the Valley Forge encampment did not cover much ground, and he'd naturally go to the same places. So we sat there on the fallen tree, your open lunch basket between us, watching him come across the drill ground. We said to each other that if he did turn out to be a man who had served there as a soldier when we did, we'd invite him to share our meal.

"But as he came across, there was something about the way he walked, the way he carried his head——He was a tall gentleman——" His breath gave out. He could not say another word.

Debby's father said solemnly, "It was General George Washington."

There was a silence. Not even Debby, always full of questions, dared to break it. The room felt as though it were filled with something much finer than words.

Finally the two men looked at each other. "Well,"

said the delegate, "he ate lunch with us, General George Washington did."

"My lunch!" murmured Debby's mother, clasping her hands.

"He said he had gone back, just the way we did. To look at the place where, that winter——"

He paused. Debby's father said, "We talked things over together, the three of us."

"Oh, how did he look? What did he say?" Debby burst out, at last.

Her father said, gently, "He looked just as he always does. You know how he looks."

He went on, still very gently, "He didn't say much." He added so quietly that he seemed to be holding his breath, "He never does."

There was a long silence Then the delegate told them. "But *plenty*." The two men smiled at each other.

And that was all Debby and her mother ever knew.

CHAPTER XV

"WE DID THE
BEST WE COULD"

AFTER THE VACATION, ALL THE DELEGATES—ALL EX-
cept the "Committee on Detail" who had been on duty
without a single day off—came back fresh and ready
for more work. If they thought a few days more would
finish things, they were mistaken. It took six weeks
more of the same sort of drudgery—re-writing some
rule that had looked all right when it was voted, but
on second thought didn't seem quite fair to everyone,
changing words here and there to make their meaning
clear beyond mistake. It was tiresome! How they
longed to go home. They didn't, now, even have the
excitement of a hot debate to carry them along . . .
except once . . . and then it was too serious to be amus-
ing. When that dispute broke out, there were a few
days when they weren't sure that all their work had
not come to nothing. It looked as though they would
break up, finally, and with a bang, and go back home,
defeated.

None of them guessed how much dynamite there was
in the question of Negro slavery—seventy years later

almost enough to wreck the Union! In the earliest days of our country, Negro slaves had been kept in all the colonies. There were never many in the north, where they did not fit into the way farms were run. There were more and more of them as you went south. But by the time of the Convention in 1787, Massachusetts had forbidden slavery and eight States allowed no new slaves to be brought inside their borders. Almost everywhere, in Virginia as well as in New Hampshire, forward-looking leaders thought it a great pity that the system had ever been started. They hoped it would die out. None of these leaders—at least none who were in the Constitutional Convention—were willing to go so far as to make laws to free the slaves already in America. Governor Randolph expressed what most of them thought, when he said he was sorry such a special property (Negro slaves) existed. But since it did exist, he supposed the right to it would have to be protected by the law, like any other property.

But bringing in new slaves from Africa in slave-ships was something else. It was well known that the Negroes suffered frightfully during the voyage. Ever so many people, nearly everybody, thought that was wrong. They wanted it to stop. And the lid blew off in the hottest quarrel of the Convention when South Carolina insisted that it be written into the Constitution that Congress should never stop the slave trade.

All the debates about this were angry. In one of the most furious ones, Mr. Martin of Maryland called slavery "Contrary to the principles of the Revolution, and dishonorable to the American character."

George Mason of Virginia called it an "infernal traffic. Slavery discourages arts and manufactures," he said. "Every master of slaves is a petty tyrant."

But the South Carolina men looked black and sat tight. Every time somebody said that the slave trade was wrong, they answered coldly that their State and northern Georgia couldn't get along without it. Their chief crops were rice and indigo. To grow these, more and more new slaves were absolutely needed, because the work and the climate killed so many Negroes that a fresh supply would have to be continuous.

"Religion and humanity have nothing to do with it," said Mr. Rutledge of South Carolina. "Interest" (by this word he meant the chance to make money) "is the governing principle with nations." And once again the terrible threat was brought out that would smash up everything they had done so far. "The only question now is," he said, "whether South Carolina and Georgia shall—or shall not—come into the Union."

Another delegate was unkind enough to point out that bringing new slaves into the country was not much worse than owning (as Mason of Virginia did) a great many slaves born in this country.

It looked hopeless. Could they possibly invent some sort of a compromise which would settle it? A compromise was devised that was really a bargain. The middle States were voted down. The extreme South got the right to import more new slaves from Africa. Not forever, for twenty years more. New England was given (as the price of their votes) a freer chance to make laws about shipping. No one was very proud or satisfied about this bargain, but at least, once more, the Convention had been kept from going to pieces on the rocks.

The next two weeks went quickly. Whole sections of the Constitution were voted with hardly any debate. It was almost as if everyone was anxious not to start any more trouble. Finally about the middle of September it was all finished. Actually, all finished. They could hardly believe it.

The last word was written. But their troubles were not over. One last action was needed—the signing of the document. Many of the delegates were sore and angry about places in the Constitution that they didn't like and had worked hard to cut out. Not one of them had had his own way entirely in the Convention. Some of them were so bitter about the times they had been voted down that it was feared they might not be willing to set their names to the great paper. And if a lot of the delegates who had actually been at the Convention didn't sign it because they didn't like parts of it, there wouldn't be much chance to get it accepted, out in the different States.

On Monday the 17th of September, they came together for the last time in the hall where they had worked so long and so hard—since the twenty-fifth of May. They were very much worried. Nobody knew yet how many of the members would refuse to sign. Could it be that at the very last, the Convention would fail?

The secretary read the Constitution aloud, in its final form. When he finished, without waiting a single minute, wise old Dr. Franklin heaved himself up on his tottery legs and started to speak. But it hurt him too much to stand. He sank back into his chair while Mr. Wilson took the written speech and read it aloud.

Like all Benjamin Franklin's speeches, there was no slam-bang hurrah about it. At first it sounded very ordinary. Then, gradually everyone began to see that, as usual, what Franklin said was full of good sense which made the problem before them seem clear and simple. "Many a time in my life," it ran, "I have been absolutely sure I was right—only to change my mind a year or two later. Some people never change their minds. They are always rather ridiculous. I once knew a lady who told me that her sister said to her, 'It's the strangest thing—whenever I get into a dispute with somebody, *I've* always been the one who was right.' "

Here he waited a moment for the laugh from the delegates which they couldn't keep back, angry and anxious though they were. He went on, "Now to tell the truth, there are several points I do not greatly like about this Constitution. That is, I do not like them now. But if I can judge from the past, it is quite likely that I will like them next year. And I am sure of this: that the combined wisdom of so many thoughtful men is certain to be sounder as a whole than anything any one of us could have written alone. So I hope each of you will join me in forgetting the little you dislike here and there in it, and show your approval of the whole effort—and really it is far better than we had any right to hope for—by signing it now, and later supporting it before the people."

Then Alexander Hamilton jumped up. "Everybody knows how different this Constitution is from the one *I* favored" (he had been all along for cutting States' Rights down to almost nothing). "But the choice, as I see it, is between no government at all—for that is what we have now—and a government that may very well turn out to be better than we now expect. I certainly shall sign."

Three delegates held back—Mason, Randolph, and Gerry—and they were not enough to prevent the Constitution being the unanimous choice of all the States represented at the Convention.

There was no cheering. It was over. They had lived through it. The Constitution had been written. It was approved and passed by vote. It was signed.

Why, they could go home! The meeting adjourned. The delegates ate their last meal together at the City Tavern. They shook hands and said goodbye soberly to one another.

There was no excitement at Debby's home either. It was not a bit like the day when they had heard the Declaration read. Their delegate came home carrying a package which, somewhat embarrassed, he gave to Debby's mother. It was a clock—a handsome clock for their living-room mantel. They never before had seen such a small dainty clock.

Then he excused himself. He must put his papers in order and pack his valise. He had secured a place on an early coach tomorrow. They would understand his leaving at once. It was a long time since he had seen his family. He went up to his room.

In the morning after breakfast, he thanked them for their hospitality. They wished him good luck. To Debby's father he said, "I'll never, so long as I live, forget that hour at Valley Forge." The two men shook hands on that memory.

The Philadelphia family stood by the door, to watch him walk down the street toward the place where the coach was to start. Halfway to the corner, he turned and came back to them. "I can't leave you good friends without saying——" He hesitated, set down his valise bulging with his extra shirts, rubbed his chin, went on, "I feel I ought to tell you that we know we made mistakes. Sometimes, I fear, we did wrong." He went on so sadly that their spirits were darkened. "There come times when it does not seem possible to do what is really right. The choice seems to be between doing what is not good and—something that would be worse. But we did the best we could."

Now he turned to Debby, and his voice was brighter. "You, my dear child—all you younger people—our trust is in you. We have provided in the Constitution for amendments—ways to correct the mistakes we did not know enough to avoid. Never forget that the Con-

"You, my dear child . . . our trust is in you."

stitution can be changed. The best people of our nation will always, generation after generation, keep trying to improve it. We who have worked so hard on it, will go down to our graves trusting that the Americans of the future will love freedom and justice as we have—and serve them better."

He took Debby's hand in his. "May you and your children, and your grandchildren—and mine—always be on the side of those who are working for more justice, and more freedom." He said this so earnestly that it sounded almost like a prayer.

He put on his hat, bowed to them all and went away—really away. They never saw him again.

But they did hear from him. Next July came a polite letter asking about their health and then, fairly boiling over with pride, "I have heard that New Hampshire has ratified the Constitution—and almost at the same time, Virginia. That makes ten States accepting our Constitution. Now the Government of the United States of America will be formed without delay."

The Spring after that a shorter note to Debby's father, beginning, "Dear Comrade:—With what joy we both learn that our former Commander-in-Chief is now President Washington."

A year and a half later, near Christmas time, he burst out in joyful relief, "One of my greatest regrets is gone. One of our greatest mistakes is corrected. The Amendments for the Bill of Rights are now part of the Constitution. Henceforth all American citizens are se-

cure in the right to free speech, free worship, fair trial
by jury. . . ."

After that, not every single year, but often, around
midsummer, a friendly note came from him, ending
with "Congratulations to Mistress Debby on her latest
birthday."

C H A P T E R   X V I

W H A T   Y O U   M I G H T
C A L L   A   P O S T S C R I P T

FIFTY-THREE YEARS AFTER DEBBY AND HER FAMILY
had said goodbye to their delegate and watched him
walk away from them down the street, the United
States Government published the notes taken down in
shorthand by Mr. Madison on the proceedings of the
Constitutional Convention in 1787. It was the first
chance anybody had ever had to know, really, com-
pletely, what had gone on in that big, hot hall in
Philadelphia, where the fate of the nation had been
decided.

Debby and her husband sent at once to Washington
to buy the three big volumes. They cost a good deal.
The price was more than they would have thought of
spending on a book, although Debby's husband had a
pretty good salary as a bank cashier. But like other
Americans of their age, they had wondered for fifty
years about the details of that Convention.

A few of the delegates as they grew older had talked
about it. Some of the discussion had been set down.
But these odds and ends of notes and memories con-

tradicted each other so heartily that not much could
be learned from them.

Now the whole official record was to be printed.
Now anybody could find out what had been kept so
secret all those years.

Debby and her husband were living out in Illinois,
having moved from place to place during the fifty years
of their marriage, as Americans do. Their children were
all grown up, and doing well, with boys and girls of
their own. The "old folks" had meant to put their extra
money that season into a new harness for the family
horse which pulled the little low chaise in which they
drove to church or to visit the married daughter who
lived in the same town.

But they did want those Madison Notes! They went
out to the barn together to look at the harness. It wasn't
so much worn as they had thought. They decided that
it could be mended, blacked up carefully, the brass
pieces polished, and do well enough for another year.

When the big package came in from Washington,
Debby was alone in the house. Her husband was down
at the bank. They had planned to go through the Notes
together, taking turns reading aloud. But Debby
couldn't wait to begin. There was one meeting of that
long-ago Convention she was specially curious about.
Why did the delegate who roomed with her family in
Philadelphia seem so low-spirited all through the first
part of July, and then suddenly one day come home
smiling with a bouquet of roses for her birthday and
say that evening that Mr. Wilson of Pennsylvania was

"an honor to the human race"? She remembered the exact date. Of course. It was her birthday, July 13th.

She opened the package of books, looked through them to see which one of the three was for July, put on her steel-rimmed reading spectacles, sat down in her favorite rocking chair, and turned to July 13th.

The entry for that day began, "It being moved to postpone the clause in the Report of the Committee of Eleven as to . . ." Why, she couldn't understand a word of it! Her heart sank. Had they wasted the harness money on something she would never be able to make any sense out of? She turned back a few pages and tried again, skimming along. Yes, when she got used to the long words it began to be easier. Some of the delegates were worried, it seemed, whether people from what was then the back country of the West might not in time take control of the government. One vote for every citizen was dangerous, they thought. Harsh words were spoken. They disagreed fiercely with one another. Property is power, ought to be power. All moonshine to let penniless frontiersmen with only an axe, a rifle and a log cabin—no matter how many there might be of them—send more representatives than the old, educated, rich Atlantic seaboard. It was voted that the number of representatives in Congress should be figured both on the number of voters *and their wealth*. The more money a State had, the more votes it was to have. That was actually voted.

Debby looked at the date. That must have been one of the dark nights their delegate walked so long and so wearily up and down their garden path. But then, on the page for July thirteenth, her eye was caught by a phrase . . . "moved to strike out the word 'wealth'." And here was Mr. Wilson's speech, here was the reason her delegate had looked so happy after having been so sad. "All men, wherever placed, have equal rights," he began. ". . . If the new western States ever have more voters, we should not, we cannot deny them their fair share of representation in Congress. . . . And finally, as for the argument of my opponents, I disagree absolutely. Property is *not* the sole or primary object of government and society. The most noble object of government is the cultivation and improvement of the

human mind." She felt her heart leap up. Mr. Wilson
had spoken for America at its best. And the delegates
had acted like the best Americans. Every single State
but one voted to strike out the word "wealth". No
wonder their delegate was proud and happy the evening of her birthday.

So that settled it . . . no, as she turned over the
page she came on another effort to keep law-making
power in the settled East. Though wealth was now
given up as a measuring rod, some of the delegates suggested writing into the Constitution a fixed rule that
no new States could ever outvote the old thirteen.

Again someone spoke for America as it was to be.
This time with the voice of old Mr. Sherman, who
started life as a shoemaker, taught himself, now represented his State. "We are providing for our children
and grandchildren," he said, "and they are as likely to
be citizens of the new States as of the old ones. I am
against any restrictions." Again the best spirit of America came to life at generous words. The vote of the
Convention sustained him. No restrictions were voted.

What did that vote mean, Debby asked herself? And
thought, joyfully, "Why, it meant free and equal government for all the States I have lived in, where my
children now live . . . Ohio, Michigan, Indiana, Illinois. They were, all of them, wild Indian and trapper
country in that hot Philadelphia summer of 1787. And
others also." She counted on her fingers. Yes, there were
thirteen new ones since the Constitution was adopted,
just double the old number, far more than double the

size. To say nothing of . . . maybe . . . who knew
. . . more to come, on the other side of the Mississippi.

What would have happened if those delegates had
not stuck at it until they put together a set of rules
that could be stretched to take in all that new country?
What a terrible mix-up if they hadn't. And how fas-
cinating it was to look at last behind those closed
doors!

She turned over page after page, not reading steadily
. . . that would come on long winter evenings . . .
but now stopping only when some striking event caught
her eye. How did it end? She opened the last volume.
Why late, late—even at the end of August it was still
uncertain. Mr. Martin was sure the people would never
accept the Constitution if they took time to think it
over. Mr. Gerry agreed. The system proposed, he
thought, was full of vices. Mr. Mason said he would
sooner chop off his right hand than sign the Constitution as it stood then. And Mr. Morris snapped back at
them, "All right, let's go home and leave everything to
another Convention that will have the courage to provide a vigorous government, which *we are afraid to do.*"

And yet they did not give up. They stayed, and as
her delegate had said, "They did the best they could."
She understood now why he had been so solemn when
he had said goodbye. After those months of strain, none
of them could be sure that their work had any value.
Her heart melted. She hoped her delegate had lived
long enough to hear the Convention spoken of as the
"Founding Fathers." Everyone called them that now.

And they deserved it. In those long, long days of debate and deep thought, they had hammered out a system which worked, which had endured, which would endure.

Drawing a long breath of relief, she looked up.

To her surprise four of her grandchildren stood there, rosy and smiling, their coats and caps still on, their skates hanging on their shoulders. Debby's ears as well as her eyes were now rather dulled by her age. She had not heard them come into the house, as they often did, after school or play, hoping for apples or cookies.

They laughed out now to see her look astonished that they were there.

"We just clumped up the stairs," they said, "but you were so deep in your reading you never heard a sound. We've been standing here watching you—almost ready to cry one minute, by your looks—and then ready to give three cheers. That must be an exciting story."

One of them leaned over her shoulder and read out the title:

"DEBATES OF THE CONSTITUTIONAL

CONVENTION IN 1787

as set down by Mr. James Madison."

The youngsters broke into groans. "Oh Granny, how *can* you read such a dull book?"

At this, to their great surprise, their grandmother broke into a merry ringing laugh, as though they had said something funny! Such a young laugh! They had never heard their grandmother laugh so like a girl.

They liked her, all right. She was always good to them, especially when one of them was sick. But she had seemed to them a very serious-minded old lady— working hard in the local Society for the Abolition of Slavery, always doing something for the public schools of town, always reading the accounts of the political goings-on in Washington, instead of the fashion notes. They were not used to seeing her enjoy a joke so heartily.

And what *was* the joke?

She pulled off her reading spectacles to see them more clearly. Her eyes were still crinkled at the corners from her laugh. "Dull!" she said, and laughed again. "It's only dull to ignorant people. It's the most exciting book I ever read in all my life!"

THE DECLARATION OF

INDEPENDENCE

Declaration of Independence

IN CONGRESS, July 4, 1776

THE UNANIMOUS DECLARATION of the thirteen united STATES OF AMERICA.

WHEN in the Course of human events, it becomes necessary for one people to dissolve the political bands which have connected them with another, and to assume among the powers of the earth, the separate and equal station to which the Laws of Nature and of Nature's God entitle them, a decent respect to the opinions of mankind requires that they should declare the causes which impel them to the separation.—We hold these truths to be self-evident, that all men are created equal, that they are endowed by their Creator with certain unalienable Rights, that among these are Life, Liberty and the pursuit of Happiness.—That to secure these rights, Governments are instituted among Men, deriving their just powers from the consent of the governed,—That whenever any Form of Government becomes destructive of these ends, it is the Right of the People to alter or to abolish it, and to institute a new Government, laying its foundation on such principles and organizing its powers in such form, as to them shall seem most likely to effect their Safety and Happiness. Prudence, indeed, will dictate that Govern-

ments long established should not be changed for light
and transient causes; and accordingly all experience hath
shewn, that mankind are more disposed to suffer, while
evils are sufferable, than to right themselves by abolishing the forms to which they are accustomed. But when a
long train of abuses and usurpations, pursuing invari-
ably the same Object evinces a design to reduce them
under absolute Despotism, it is their right, it is their
duty, to throw off such Government, and to provide new
Guards for their future security.—Such has been the
patient sufferance of these Colonies; and such is now the
necessity which constrains them to alter their former
Systems of Government. The history of the present King
of Great Britain is a history of repeated injuries and
usurpations, all having in direct object the establishment
of an absolute Tyranny over these States. To prove this,
let Facts be submitted to a candid world.—He has refused his Assent to Laws, the most wholesome and
necessary for the public good.—He has forbidden his
Governors to pass Laws of immediate and pressing im-
portance, unless suspended in their operation till his Assent should be obtained; and when so suspended, he has
utterly neglected to attend to them.—He has refused to
pass other Laws for the accommodation of large districts
of people, unless those people would relinquish the right
of Representation in the Legislature, a right inestimable
to them and formidable to tyrants only.—He has called
together legislative bodies at places unusual, uncom-
fortable, and distant from the depository of their public
Records, for the sole purpose of fatiguing them into com-
pliance with his measures.—He has dissolved Representative Houses repeatedly, for opposing with manly

firmness his invasions on the rights of the people.—He
has refused for a long time, after such dissolutions, to
cause others to be elected; whereby the Legislative
Powers, incapable of Annihilation, have returned to the
People at large for their exercise; the State remaining in
the mean time exposed to all the dangers of invasion
from without, and convulsions within.—He has endeavoured to prevent the population of these States; for that
purpose obstructing the Laws for Naturalization of
Foreigners; refusing to pass others to encourage their
migrations hither, and raising the conditions of new Ap-
propriations of Lands.—He has obstructed the Admin-
istration of Justice, by refusing his Assent to Laws for
establishing Judiciary Powers.—He has made Judges dependent on his Will alone, for the tenure of their offices,
and the amount and payment of their salaries. He has
erected a multitude of New Offices, and sent hither
swarms of Officers to harass our people, and eat out their
substance.—He has kept among us, in times of peace,
Standing Armies without the Consent of our legislatures.
—He has affected to render the Military independent of
and superior to the Civil Power.—He has combined with
others to subject us to a jurdisdiction foreign to our
constitution, and unacknowledged by our laws; giving
his Assent to their Acts of pretended Legislation:—For
quartering large bodies of armed troops among us:—
For protecting them, by a mock Trial, from punishment
for any Murders which they should commit on the Inhabitants of these States:—For cutting off our Trade
with all parts of the world:—For imposing Taxes on us
without our Consent:—For depriving us in many cases,
of the benefits of Trial by Jury:—For transporting us

beyond Seas to be tried for pretended offences:—For abolishing the free System of English Laws in a neighbouring Province, establishing therein an Arbitrary government, and enlarging its Boundaries so as to render it at once an example and fit instrument for introducing the same absolute rule into these Colonies:—For taking away our Charters, abolishing our most valuable Laws and altering fundamentally the Forms of our Governments:—For suspending our own Legislatures, and declaring themselves invested with power to legislate for us in all cases whatsoever.—He has abdicated Government here, by declaring us out of his Protection and waging War against us.—He has plundered our seas, ravaged our Coasts, burnt our towns, and destroyed the lives of our people.—He is at this time transporting large Armies of foreign Mercenaries to compleat the works of death, desolation and tyranny, already begun with circumstances of Cruelty & perfidy scarcely paralleled in the most barbarous ages, and totally unworthy the Head of a civilized nation.—He has constrained our fellow Citizens taken Captive on the high Seas to bear Arms against their Country, to become the executioners of their friends and Brethren, or to fall themselves by their Hands.—He has excited domestic insurrections amongst us, and has endeavoured to bring on the inhabitants of our frontiers, the merciless Indian Savages, whose known rule of warfare, is an undistinguished destruction of all ages, sexes and conditions. In every stage of these Oppressions We have Petitioned for Redress in the most humble terms: Our repeated Petitions have been answered only by repeated injury. A Prince, whose character is thus marked by every act which may define a Tyrant, is unfit to be the ruler of a free people. Nor have We been wanting in attentions to our British brethren. We have warned them, from time to time, of attempts by their legislature to extend an unwarrantable jurisdiction over us. We have reminded them of the circumstances of our emigration and settlement here. We have appealed to their native justice and magnanimity, and we have conjured them by the ties of our common kindred to disavow these usurpations, which would inevitably interrupt our connections and correspondence. They too have been deaf to the voice of justice and of consanguinity. We must, therefore, acquiesce in the necessity, which denounces our Separation, and hold them, as we hold the rest of mankind, Enemies in War, in Peace Friends.—

WE, THEREFORE, the Representatives of the UNITED STATES OF AMERICA, in General Congress, Assembled, appealing to the Supreme Judge of the world for the rectitude of our intentions, do, in the Name, and by Authority of the good People of these Colonies, solemnly publish and declare, That these United Colonies are, and of Right ought to be FREE AND INDEPENDENT STATES: that they are Absolved from all Allegiance to the British Crown, and that all political connection between them and the State of Great Britain, is and ought to be totally dissolved; and that as Free and Independent States, they have full Power to levy War, conclude Peace, contract Alliances, establish Commerce, and to do all other Acts and Things which Independent States may of right do.—And for the support of this Declaration, with a firm reliance on the protection of Divine Providence, we mutually pledge

to each other our Lives, our Fortunes and our sacred
Honor.

John Hancock
Button Gwinnett
Lyman Hall
Geo. Walton
Wm. Hooper
Joseph Hewes
John Penn
Edward Rutledge
Thos. Heyward, Jr.
Thomas Lynch, Jr.
Arthur Middleton
Samuel Chase
Wm. Paca
Thos. Stone
Charles Carroll of
    Carrollton
George Wythe
Richard Henry Lee
Th. Jefferson
Benj. Harrison

Thos. Nelson, Jr.
Francis Lightfoot
    Lee
Carter Braxton
Robt. Morris
Benjamin Rush
Benj. Franklin
John Morton
Geo. Clymer
Jas. Smith
Geo. Taylor
James Wilson
Geo. Ross
Caesar Rodney
Geo. Read
Tho. M:Kean
Wm. Floyd
Phil. Livingston
Frans. Lewis

Lewis Morris
Richd. Stockton
Jno. Witherspoon
Fras. Hopkinson
John Hart
Abra. Clark
Josiah Bartlett
Wm. Whipple
Saml. Adams
John Adams
Robt. Treat Paine
Elbridge Gerry
Step. Hopkins
William Ellery
Roger Sherman
Sam. Huntington
Wm. Williams
Oliver Wolcott
Matthew Thornton